Hidden by the Brook

by J. K. Sanchez

Unless otherwise indicated all scripture quotations are taken from The ESV Bible (The Holy Bible, English Standard Version).

Scripture quotations are from The ESV Bible (The Holy Bible, English Standard Version®), copyright © 2001 by Crossway, a publishing ministry of Good News Publishers. Used by permission. All rights reserved.

Scripture quotations marked (TPT) are from The Passion Translation®. Copyright © 2017, 2018 by Passion & Fire Ministries, Inc. Used by permission. All rights reserved. ThePassionTranslation.com.

Hidden by the Brook: Finding Hope in Uncertainty

ISBN – 978-0-578-84480-0

Copyright © 2021 by J. K. Sanchez. Published by: Button Lane Books Spanaway, WA 98387

Contact: www.jksanchez.com or jksanchez.author@gmail.com

Cover Photography by: Donna Jackson

Cover Design by: J.K Sanchez Photography and Button Lane Books

Printed in the United States of America. All rights reserved under International Copyright Law. Contents and/or cover may not be reproduced in whole or in part in any form without the express written consent of the Author

Dedication

To those who find themselves in the midst of life's *waiting process,* I encourage you to not give up nor lose hope. You are not alone, God has a plan for you to shine forth His glory. Trust in His faithfulness as you allow his transforming power to draw you to an undistracted place at the feet of Jesus Christ.

Table of Contents

	Introduction	iii
Chapter 1	**Hidden to Bring Deliverance**	1
	Stories from the Life of Moses	
Chapter 2	**Hidden to Turn a Nation**	27
	Stories from the Life of Elijah	
Chapter 3	**Hidden for an Eternal Plan**	47
	Stories from the Life of Jesus	
Chapter 4	**Hidden to Preserve Life**	71
	Stories from the Life of Joseph	
Chapter 5	**Hidden to Spread the Gospel**	99
	Stories from the Life of Paul	
Chapter 6	**Hidden to Become King**	121
	Stories from the Life of David	
Chapter 7	**Hidden for God's Perfect Timing**	149
	Stories from the Lives of Esther, Noah and Jonah	
Chapter 8	**Hidden to Come Forth**	173
	Stories of Victory Found in Hidden Places	

Acknowledgments

First and foremost, I am thankful for the support and consistent overflow of love from my husband, Dennis, my children, their spouses and my grandchildren. My overwhelming Joy is found in each of your faces.

Another huge "Thank you" to Amber Lynn Sanchez for all your hours of passionate commitment to editing every letter, phrase and comma – and so much more!

My continued love and appreciation to my sister, Donna Jackson. Your beautiful photography takes my breath away. Thank you for sharing it with me to accomplish this cover.

And finally – but above all – my thanks to Jesus Christ who directed, inspired, and taught me to enter the hidden times with hope and anticipation of His plans for my life – not my own. I am thankful to walk daily in His peace and assurance of His love. His presence and promise of favor and abundance are always there for me.

My life is not my own but a gift freely given back to the one who gave His life for me.

Introduction

The bible is filled with stories of men and women who were used by God in impactful, life-changing ways. But found within the pages of their life stories, you will find times of isolation – hidden times – where they were required to make choices, completely trust God and walk into new, frightening paths that would change history.

You will experience difficult times – hidden times – in your life story, too. In these times, despondency and questions may cause you to lose hope. Your choices will be no different than the choices made by individuals that you will find in the stories of this little book; each had to accept, yield and forge ahead into a *new normal*.

Whenever your life is interrupted, be aware that God has a plan and purpose. These times come upon all of us – times of unplanned, instantaneous change that disrupt everything we know as *normal*. How we walk through the storm is the key to triumphant hope. Just as Jonah and Saul, we will need to humbly go to our knees, surrender our thoughts, opinions and desires, cry out in prayer and trust in God's plan – not ours. It is at this place that we will acknowledge His ways over our own and stand up to walk in the purposes God has planned for us.

Hope tells us that God always has the best waiting for us and that there is a great future available and coming. When that hope is tested, something remarkable happens: it changes from mere agreement into belief. In this place, you now can say, "Yes, Lord." The presence of a deep reliance and confidence in Jesus Christ now resides within you – He is the one that you know you can trust and have set your hope and belief in. Somewhere in that testing, in the <u>hidden waiting process</u>, your belief will shift into faith. Faith tells us that all we have been hoping for is available and here for us now. It is in the midst of the greatest difficulties that we find faith – a living and active faith – that will allow us to confidently step into the fiery furnace or the lion's den, knowing God is in control, no matter the outcome.

God's plan for your life is not one lived in hopelessness – but one filled with abundance. His plan for every life is to see a surrendered and prepared vessel. This comes to completion when a willing heart surrenders during the <u>waiting process</u> of life's difficult circumstances. In this yielded place, the willing heart will now reach out to Him for hope and direction. Here, transformation occurs as "Yes, Lord," is declared and His planned assignment is accepted. Now, with the confidence and boldness that only comes from a relationship where abiding at the foot of the cross has been cultivated, movement forward into a life of abundance is possible.

<u>Where does that triumphant hope come from?</u>

It is found in knowing:

- You are not forgotten (He is always with you and comes alongside you).
- You have been chosen (He created you and loves you).
- You have been set apart (He has a specific purpose you were created for).
- You have been gloriously sprinkled by His blood (He died for your sins).

- You have been showered with a fountain of mercy (He gives you a new life).
- You have been given a perfect, unperishable inheritance (He has released a *kingly* inheritance to you, His child).

1 Pet. 1:2-4 *you are not forgotten*, for you have been chosen and destined by Father God. The Holy Spirit has set you apart to be God's holy ones, obedient followers of Jesus Christ who have been *gloriously* sprinkled with his blood. May God's delightful grace and peace cascade over you many times over! Celebrate with praises the God and Father of our Lord Jesus Christ, who has shown us his extravagant mercy. For his *fountain of* mercy has given us a new life— we are reborn to experience a living, energetic hope through the resurrection of Jesus Christ from the dead. We are reborn into a perfect inheritance that can never perish, never be defiled, and never diminish. It is promised and preserved forever in the heavenly realm for you! (TPT)

My desire is that you find hope in your own uncertainty as you walk through these fictional depictions of some favorite Bible characters and their stories. See with new eyes how God hid them away for a time as He pulled everyday distractions away and prepared them for the great purposes He had in store. Expect your faith to be stirred and your heart to be humbled as you learn to surrender to His timing and control, not your own. Anticipate His specific *God-ordained* assignment to be revealed as you prepare your heart at the foot of the cross.

Chapter 1

Hidden to Bring Deliverance

Prov. 3:5-6 Trust in the Lord with all your heart, and do not lean on your own understanding. In all your ways acknowledge him, and he will make straight your paths.

Hidden to Bring Deliverance

Stories from the Life of Moses

The life of Moses was filled with multiple times of hiding, all directed by the very hand of God. From birth to the Egyptian court and from the desert to the wilderness, God used times of hiding to strengthen and prepare him for each phase of special anointing and great purpose. Ultimately, He used him to move His people into a life of freedom; giving them the ability to worship God freely and to walk into God's promised land.

We see God's hand all throughout the life of Moses. He was born at a tumultuous time in history – he was hidden and protected for just the right time. Raised among those who would eventually desire to kill him, he was given education, privilege and leadership training. Hidden again in the desert, he learned valuable life lessons that prepared him to be used by God's mighty hand. Then, once again, he was hidden in the wilderness as he led, taught and raised up a nation to know and worship God.

Each stage of his life he stayed hidden until God's planned timeline, and God took care of him. God provided everything he needed as He prepared him for His glorious purpose: to deliver His people, show them who God is and raise them back up to be people with hearts that would follow their God.

A Faith-Filled Mother

*P*ain seared through her body as each contraction drew her closer to the time of delivery. What normally should have been a time of great joy and anticipation, was instead shrouded in fear. The current political climate was filled with aggravation and turmoil, as the pharaoh declared all male babies to be drowned in the river. Jochebed found her mind wondering to the stories, tears and grief that had been shared at the well every morning; stories that stirred fear within her as her belly had continued to grow with new life.

Her internal questions ceaselessly swirled, "If it's a girl, life will be normal – but if it's a boy, how do I survive that loss? What can I do?" The horrible memories of the sounds of her friends and neighbors as they succumbed with grief-stricken screams while their sons were ripped from their arms and drowned in the river upon birth – these only heightened her fears as the next contraction brought her attention to the present.

The internal and external struggle raged on, hour after hour, as thoughts and fears surfaced repeatedly, "What if my baby is a son? How can I possibly keep him safe?"

Those thoughts would have to be quickly set aside, as yet another contraction erupted from within – each one drawing her closer to the answer.

The shrill, tiny cry caused her heart to soar. Even in the midst of fear, she could not help but feel joy overwhelm her as this new life entered the world. Looking upon his beautiful face and taking him into her arms, she knew God had blessed her. But she must trust that her God would keep him safe.

This little gift was hers for now; she would love him, care for him and protect him, trusting God all the while.

As several months passed, he grew stronger, bigger and louder, and she knew that in order to protect him she would have to trust God in a much bigger way. Her faith was again being challenged as she realized that all of this hiding could all be for naught if he was found now. A difficult decision soon had to be made before the choice was stripped from her arms by the pharaoh's men. If her son had to be placed in the river, she would be the one to do it and trust her God to be in control of his destiny. As a Hebrew Levite, she believed in God's control – but here in this personal place of anguish, her trust was stretched beyond what she had been taught.

Jochebed prepared a basket that would float, covering every opening with tar. She carefully wrapped him, placed him into the basket and carried him to the river. With her daughter following along, they said their goodbyes and carefully slipped the basket into the bulrushes as the current lifted and moved him into the river. Heavy-hearted, she returned home while her daughter watched and followed to see where the basket carrying her baby brother would go. She watched as he floated up to the place where the pharaoh's daughter was bathing, and, with great anticipation, saw him rescued from the river.

Jochebed's daughter boldly stepped into the scene, and as her brother began to cry, she offered to find a Hebrew mother to nurse him. Running home with excitement, she burst through the door expressing God's faithfulness as she told her mother the great news. God had provided!

God had kept her son safe and would now allow her to continue to care for her sweet baby boy under the guise of being his nursemaid.
(Enjoy reading the whole story in Ex. 2:1-10)

God's wisdom and direction in the midst of uncertainty requires an ear tuned to His voice and the confidence to step out. When He directs, there is purpose involved – and we rarely understand or know what that ultimate purpose is until we are on the other side of it.

As we look at this well-known Bible story, the life of Moses, we normally focus only on Moses and not on his mother. We aren't told much about this brave, faith-filled woman of God. But her response to the challenges, her decisions and her patient trust in God brought about the great purpose of Moses.

Jochebed was no different than you and I. When the time came for her to choose what to do, she had to trust that her thoughts and directions were coming from God. We don't always know – we just believe. And so, it was with her, as she stepped out and tried something to save her baby. Preparation was necessary. The making of the basket – weaving and covering it with tar to keep it afloat. Perhaps she had spent time observing the women at the river and saw their times of bathing as a possibility for the rescue of her son. During all the preparations, the heaviness of her heart and the knowledge that she had to let him go stood daily in front of her. The overwhelming "mother's love" inside, drove her to a faith that she never thought possible –

a trust that God had given her this beautiful son – and she would do all she could to save him and then trust God to "show up."

This is just a fictional story, of course, since we know so little about Jochebed – but it is a story that resonates with us now in our current political and social upheaval. It tells us that in the midst of hiding we need to keep our ears tuned to God's wisdom and directions, stay sheltered until He says, "it is time," and be willing to step out even at great sacrifice.

The time of hiding is not a time of inactivity; it is a time of nourishment and growth. It is in these times that our roots become strong in order to withstand what is to come. It is a time to learn endurance. It is at this time, when all of life becomes quiet that we can reset our hearts and minds. This reset allows us to focus on the Word of God, His presence, and we can lean in close to listen intently for His voice – not the voices that surround us.

Summary thought:

Becoming a brave, faith-filled follower of Christ, one who is able to respond to the challenges and decisions we need to make, will always require a patient trust in God. We must, like Jochebed, be stretched beyond what has been our understanding. We must not dwell on what was the "past normal," but look for His hand over our situation and look forward to a "new normal." We must trust that He is in control and has a greater purpose in store for us.

Ps. 62:8 Trust in him at all times, O people; pour out your heart before him; God is a refuge for us.

Rom. 12:12 Rejoice in hope, be patient in tribulation, be constant in prayer.

Prov. 2:6 Wisdom is a gift from a generous God, and every word he speaks is full of revelation and becomes a fountain of understanding within you.

Personal Insights:
_____
_____
_____
_____
_____
_____

H: How Does this Apply to Me?
_____
_____
_____
_____

O: Observations:
_____
_____
_____
_____

P: Personal Prayer:
_____
_____
_____
_____

E: Expression Through My Life (Action Step):
_____
_____
_____
_____

Fleeing into the Desert

*I*ndignation rose within Moses as he surveyed the excruciatingly hard work these Hebrews were required to endure. The dichotomy of living conditions and the abusive treatment that were poured out on the Hebrew people caused an overwhelming culture shock to his understanding. He had no idea what his adoptive father, the pharaoh, required from these Hebrews. Their hard work and very lives were what allowed him to live in great ease and luxury. The surge of guilt swam before his eyes.

On this fateful day, he had been sent to tour what would soon be his to oversee. His previous mindset quickly began to slide into an internal upheaval as he observed the scene that unfolded before him. His eyes burned and he nearly retched as he was overcome with the smells of filth. His heart pounded inside his chest at the obvious lack of human decency that surrounded him.

Without understanding, a hurricane rose up within him; one that would bring a life-changing paradigm shift. From this day forward, he would not see the Hebrew people the same.

He was required to walk among the slaves, week after week, never growing accustom to the suffering he saw. The day arrived where he could no longer stay quiet, suddenly, he saw a soldier begin to beat a poor, hungry and broken old man, and he was driven to an outburst of violence that he quickly realized would change his life forever. Righteous anger soared within him; in a momentous burst of power, he had rescued this old man from being beaten but had killed a soldier of the king at the same time. He found that in that single reactive moment, forty years of his life had been instantly eradicated. His upbringing within the royal courts, his position and possessions and every educational advantage disappeared in one single choice – suddenly he was being driven into the desert, running for his life. Everything he had known was gone.

The scorching heat of the sun drove Moses further into the desert. Soon his stomach began to stir in need of substance, but still he moved forward. Days into his journey, he was exhausted, thirsty and hungry. A well materialized in the distance, and he moved toward a place of refreshing. He desperately needed a chance to quench his thirst and rest awhile. As he neared the well, he encountered several women needing assistance to get water for their sheep. Other shepherds stood harassing them, and he simply stepped in to help.

It was a chance meeting at this well that would provide a new opportunity for him – a new life. It was in this new life that he would find many blessings and a wonderful wife and family. Here he would come to believe and know his God, and this new life would catapult him into the beginning of forty years of desert training.

(Enjoy reading the whole story in Ex. 2:11-22)

While Moses worked in the fields, cared and tended the flocks, found love, married and fathered children, he was learning valuable lessons that God would use when the time was right.

Our society of young adults think when they turn thirty, they'd better know where they are going; when they turn forty, they are over-the-hill and that life is all downhill from there. But, more likely, our true mission in life is still out there ahead of us. It takes decades of living life, allowing God to intervene, direct and correct much of our thinking to bring us to a yielded and useable place.

Moses quickly found that out in the desert there were no more servants to care for him and meet his every need. He had to work, sweat and harden up those un-calloused hands. He learned to fight the environment and nature, as heat stole the life from crops and predators snuck in and picked off the sheep. Everything he needed had to be taken care of, and those he loved had to be fought for.

Many valuable changes took place as Moses lived those forty years in the desert; changes that molded him into a man that God could trust and speak to. These changes could only occur during a time of hiding, a time of separation from what had been a normal life. Patience was tilled into an impatient heart. Insufficiency brought down pride. Unconditional love and self-sacrifice were found. Tenacity rose into faith and hope. And, above all, faith became deeper understanding of God's control – not man's.

As we look into our lives and the months or years of exile that we have been through (those times when we feel like we have been set aside and are just treading water), consider what God may be tempering into your life. He may need to till in some patience, bring down some pride, show you unconditional love or teach you self-sacrifice.

Adjustments are needed for you to move forward into the next phase of your life: where His ultimate desire is for faith in Christ to rise up and become the main focus driving you into the place where His call – your purpose – is walked into. The place where your life will be useable to bring freedom to others.

Summary thought:

Willingly yield into where God has placed you right now. Allow the Holy Spirit to take and use the circumstances in your life to humble and adjust your thoughts, attitudes and desires.

Accept and move forward into a place where your current life can be reset to the plans and purposes of God's plan – not your own. This humble willingness will set the stage for what He has waiting for you. A willing, yielded spirit in the midst of your hidden time is what will be required.

James 4:10 Humble yourself before the Lord, and He will exalt you.

Ps. 46:10 Surrender your anxiety! Be silent and stop your striving and you will see that I am God. I am the God above all the nations, and I will be exalted throughout the whole earth. (TPT)

Rom. 5:3-4 But that's not all! Even in times of trouble we have a joyful confidence, knowing that our pressures will develop in us patient endurance. And patient endurance will refine our character, and proven character leads us back to hope. (TPT)

Personal Insights:
_____
_____
_____
_____
_____
_____
_____

H: How Does this Apply to Me?
_____
_____
_____
_____

O: Observations:
_____
_____
_____
_____

P: Personal Prayer:
_____
_____
_____
_____

E: Expression Through My Life (Action Step):
_____
_____
_____
_____

"Yes, Lord!"

Spending hours in the desert had brought Moses much peace. It was here that he had found his heart, mind and soul being taught by God. Here he learned that this God is the only true God. He thought, that somehow, out here in the dark loneliness of the desert, that he had come to know Him – maybe have somewhat of a friendship with Him. But on this dark night, an unexplainable presence seemed to surround him, as a desert scrub bush suddenly burst into flame – yet it was not being consumed. And just as suddenly, a voice began to speak to him from within the bush.

He wondered, "What is this strange sight and sound? Is this God?"

As the voice told him to remove his shoes, he found himself on shaking knees and bare feet. Now kneeling in front of a burning bush, his mind swirled with questions and unbelief as he watched this fire blazing – yet not consuming the bush that it engulfed.

"How can this be?" he asked.

But then the voice spoke again from within the bush, and fear pushed him to comprehend that this was God! The words he heard made no sense, God was asking him – a simple sheep herder; a husband; a father; an average normal guy – to free His people from slavery.

Stirring with great fear and wonder, his mind contemplated, "Why would God use me for such an astonishing task? I know who I am and know that I am not worthy of anything so great – I cannot even speak with fluency."

Even with all these doubts saturating his consciousness, it was obvious that God had other plans. Doubt was soon removed, as God told him to pick up a stick and throw it down. Where the stick was laid, suddenly a snake slithered on the ground. Then he was instructed to pick it up again by the tail and it instantly was returned to a stick. <u>*Now*</u> *Moses understood the power that God was sending him out with, and his little faith was just enough to answer God's request with a humble, "Yes, Lord."*

After forty years of hiding in the desert, he was now being asked to go back to Egypt – back to where he had been forced to run for his life from the very people who had raised him. The emotional struggles, fears and memories all surged within him. But God is never wrong in His timeline, His preparation or His purpose. So, after hearing and accepting God's call, he stepped into the supernatural realm of the Almighty as he obediently moved forward and watched the deliverance of the Hebrew people transpire. Unexpected miracle after miracle materialized as Moses stretched out a simple stick.

Plague after plague poured out, the splitting of the sea for a crossing, the elimination of an army, provision of goods, food and water for a multitude – these were just the beginning as the Hebrew nation journeyed into freedom and toward God's promised land.

But due to rebellion within the nation, Moses soon found that there would be one more time of hiding for him – a final forty.

Forty more years as he would teach and lead this nation. Teaching them to love the Lord their God and to worship Him ONLY.

Forty more years preparing them to receive God's Promised Land and to walk into it with faith in who He is!

(Enjoy the whole story in Ex.3-Deut.3)

After forty years in the desert, Moses had become the man God intended to use. A simple man, yet a man with a humble, moldable, willing heart to serve his God.

God's timeline is always the right one. His preparation of our heart does not mean the same for any one person. As we find ourselves hidden and isolated away (whether in the natural or emotional), God desires us to allow Him to adjust every area that needs to be humbled and readied for His use. Only then will we be ready to move forward when He calls.

Moses was quickly tested when God called him to step out of his comfort zone – his safe place where he had been hidden, the place he had become accustomed to. The internal struggle, the discussions with family, the questions and ridicule from the community; all of these saturated the natural fibers of his being. But in the end, he had to make the choice; he had to know what God said was true, and he was the only one who would need to say, "Yes, Lord."

Choice is always part of the plan of God; any time He calls us, there is a choice we must make. He requires a willing step of faith made from a heart of love – not compulsion. The bigger the call, the bigger the choice – and greater the cost. So it was with Moses, too. He had to say, "YES, Lord," willingly.

The cost would require leaving his home, stepping into a life-threatening environment and becoming someone, he knew he was not! Believing that God was on his side and preparing the way still required him to move into that call. He had to choose to step out of hiding into his great purpose.

Being hidden away can take a day, a month, a year – or as with Moses, forty years. Fighting against the place of refuge is to defeat what God wants to do within you. However, when He calls you to step out (even if you don't feel ready), the choice still has to be made – and it sits squarely on you to make that choice.

The key in making that choice is to spend time at the feet of Jesus as you wait in this secluded, *waiting process*. Allow Him to shower you with His presence, speak to you through the Holy Spirit's revelations and drink in the wisdom and understanding that can only be found in the Word of God. These will change your heart. You will become moldable and willing as you are humbled at His feet. You will become not who you think you should be, but who He says you are. Once God has completed His purpose within you, He will be the one to decide that you are ready and then His call to move forward will come. Then, and only then, our choice will either be one of retreat – back into that safe place – or a humble, shaky response of, "Yes, Lord."

Summary thought:

As we live in the midst of the chaos and life circumstances that surround us, being tuned in to the voice of God on a daily basis will drive us forward.

Transformation through His revelations, together with our choices, will bring us to a humble place at His feet and allow us to respond to His directions with a "Yes, Lord," response, even if it is still somewhat doubtful or shaky.

Step forward into what He directs with confidence in Him who calls you.

---

2 Chron. 33:12 And when he was in distress, he entreated the favor of the Lord his God and humbled himself greatly before the God of his fathers.

Ps. 51:12 Let my passion for life be restored, tasting joy in every breakthrough you bring to me. Hold me close to you with a willing spirit that obeys whatever you say. (TPT)

Josh. 24:15 And if it is evil in your eyes to serve the Lord, choose this day whom you will serve, whether the gods your fathers served in the region beyond the River, or the gods of the Amorites in whose land you dwell. But as for me and my house, we will serve the Lord."

Personal Insights:
_____
_____
_____
_____
_____
_____
_____

H: How Does this Apply to Me?
_____
_____
_____
_____

O: Observations:
_____
_____
_____
_____

P: Personal Prayer:
_____
_____
_____
_____

E: Expression Through My Life (Action Step):
_____
_____
_____
_____

One-in-a-Million

*T*he Israelites rejoiced as they experienced God's mighty hand of deliverance, but their memories grew dull, as day after day, they trudged through the desert. God continued to provide for them and lead them with a cloud by day and a pillar of fire at night, but these miracles became commonplace in their hearts and minds. Complaining rose up before God like an offering, but this one had an unpleasant aroma.

Years passed as Moses led the nation; instilling laws and guidance, placing God as the one and only true God continually before the Hebrew people, building a tabernacle to worship before the Lord and imparting times and seasons of worship. Yet the grumbling grew and division stirred within the camp.

As God directed, Moses sent spies out into the land that God had promised for the Israelites to occupy. Upon their return, hope rose again as bountiful loads of produce were carried into the camp. However, negative reports stirred fears within the congregation. The reports spoke of how big and mighty their adversaries were and that they surely would not be able to overcome these powerful men. They spoke without faith, doubting that what God had declared could belong to them. Two faith-filled men proclaimed that this land was flowing with milk and honey, just as God had said, and that He would go with them to take the land of promise. But doubt prevailed; a great sound of grumbling rose before God and His heart was angered.

For forty years the Hebrew nation wandered, missing out on God's land of milk and honey. They were kept hidden away from the promise because of their doubt and fear.

The ungrateful, fearful, doubting response of the Israelites caused God's promised land to be unseen by the living generation, except for the faith-filled two. Those two who believed that God would deliver the land into their hands where "one in a million," – they were the ones able to walk into the promised land.

(Enjoy reading the whole story in Num. 13-14)

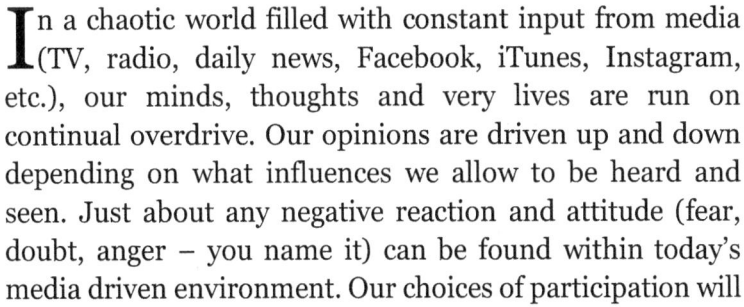

In a chaotic world filled with constant input from media (TV, radio, daily news, Facebook, iTunes, Instagram, etc.), our minds, thoughts and very lives are run on continual overdrive. Our opinions are driven up and down depending on what influences we allow to be heard and seen. Just about any negative reaction and attitude (fear, doubt, anger – you name it) can be found within today's media driven environment. Our choices of participation will direct our opinions and emotions.

God does not ask us our opinions; He asks us to believe Him. We stand on what the Word of God tells us – not man or media.

Today, we stand much like the camp of Israel who chose to listen to the negative reports about "how big and mighty our adversaries are." We often choose to believe man's opinions, and not the promise of abundant life that God promises through Christ.

Your choice to believe God over the constant, negative murmuring around you will determine your ability to walk into the promised land. As you believe and continue to stand, trusting only in God, you will be kept in peace while you wait for God's timing to bring you out of a hidden place.

Keeping your focus on listening to positive God-driven input, reading the Word of God, waiting in His presence and lifting worship before the throne will keep you filled with hope and faith that will move you to the exact place where God has planned for you to be.

Summary thought:

Your choice is simply to believe that He is in control, willingly giving up your own opinions and laying down your emotions. Then you can become that "one-in-a-million" believer that KNOWS God is for you and will beat back the giants on your behalf. The choice is yours.

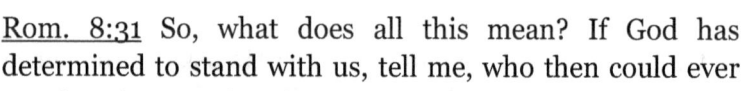

Rom. 8:31 So, what does all this mean? If God has determined to stand with us, tell me, who then could ever stand against us? (TPT)

Prov. 3:5-6 Trust in the Lord completely, and do not rely on your own opinions. With all your heart rely on him to guide you, and he will lead you in every decision you make. Become intimate with him in whatever you do, and he will lead you wherever you go. (TPT)

Heb. 12:2 We look away from the natural realm and we fasten our gaze onto Jesus who birthed faith within us and who leads us forward into faith's perfection. His example is this: Because his heart was focused on the joy of knowing that you would be his, he endured the agony of the cross and conquered its humiliation, and now sits exalted at the right hand of the throne of God! (TPT)

Personal Insights:
_____
_____
_____
_____
_____
_____

H: How Does this Apply to Me?
_____
_____
_____
_____

O: Observations:
_____
_____
_____
_____

P: Personal Prayer:
_____
_____
_____
_____

E: Expression Through My Life (Action Step):
_____
_____
_____
_____

Chapter 2

Hidden to Turn a Nation

Ps. 27:14 Wait for the Lord; be strong, and let your heart take courage;

wait for the Lord!

Hidden to Turn a Nation

Stories from the Life of Elijah

With social unrest, national leadership upheaval, disease and famine, judgement and lawlessness, anger and natural disasters surrounding us; we cry out against them as our "normal" has been drastically changed. Yet, these same issues surrounded Elijah while God saw, allowed and even encouraged a three-year drought that would cause great distress on the nation. God loved this nation so much and desired that they worship Him and Him only. His greatest purpose was for His people to call out to Him. They needed to see that man's ways, ideas and opinions were not helping him, but destroying him.

Here we sit in the same environment, complaining about the time frame that sits before us, demanding from man an answer – when the answer is not in man, but in focusing our eyes on our healer, our deliverer, our provider, on the one who came to set us free: Jesus Christ.

Elijah was set aside by the direction and hand of God – hidden by the brook – for a purpose. A purpose that would require him to step out of his everyday life, come to a humble place on his knees, cry out in prayer for the nation and trust in God's plan – and not in man's.

God Provides

King after king reigned in Israel, each continually sinking deeper into unimaginable sin. The sin rose before the Lord, and He began to stir His prophets to action. As Ahab took reign with his wife Jezebel, God said, "no more," and called a single prophet to confront him.

Elijah knew the voice of God well! However, this time as God began to reveal His plan and purpose to him, he had to calm his heart as fear tried to raise its head. He was a little hesitant to take this prediction of a devastating three-year drought before this evil king. He knew that once he approached the king with this prophesy, his life would be worthless unless God stepped in to protect him. In faith, he chose to trust and obey the voice that he had grown to know so profusely.

Just like he had considered: upon his audience with the king his life was instantly at risk. The declaration of God's intent to shut off all dew and rain for the next three years – causing a disastrous drought – was not met with a positive response, but one as evil as the king himself. Death was declared against this prophet, as well as all the prophets of Israel. The fact that Elijah made it out of the throne room alive was a feat in itself.

To protect him, God spoke to him again, promising. "Go and hide yourself by the brook and I will take care of you."

The brook was filled with fresh running water, natures rustle stirred in the air as peace and quiet saturated the environment. It was a cool resting place for him to wait for God. Elijah sat by this secluded brook for many days, hidden away from the danger surrounding him, enjoying the rest and safety it provided.

At first, he was unsure if this place would be safe and unsure if he had heard right, and certainly unsure of what was to come. But he knew the voice of God and trusted His direction – so there he sat, resting and waiting.

He was still amazed as he thought back to that first day when the ravens arrived, in the morning and in the evening, bringing him bread and meat – just as God had said. He trusted that God's plan for him was not yet complete, so he continued to wait. Being content to daily drink from this brook and eat what the ravens provided, he waited. He rested and intently listened for the call of his Lord.

Day after day marched on with no moisture, dew or rain – just as God had said. The lush trees that surrounded the brook began to show the lack of water and the bubbling brook shrank. As it continued to dry up, the brook became a narrow creek, moving slower and slower.

Days became weeks, weeks became months, and the brook grew minuscule, leaving dry rocks where the riverbed had once been. A year soon arrived, and his faith quivered as he listened for Gods next direction.

His mind questioned, "Am I to stay here and die? What is God's plan for me?"

Waiting became more difficult as his mind began to think and search for his own possible strategies to survive. Time and time again, Elijah would need to calm the fear that would begin to rise up. He knew that his God was always faithful – so when fears and doubts would surface, he would draw in closer to listen for a whisper of his Lord's direction for his life.

(Enjoy reading the whole story in 1 Kings 17:1-7)

During this time of global pandemic, we have all experienced isolation, being separated from those we love and the loss of activities that we once enjoyed. Life changed overnight – and with that change, loss and fear have risen, as hopelessness insidiously slipped in. But there is a purpose in this place of seclusion.

Let's look at God's hand of protection over Elijah. As a prophet of God, Elijah declared a three-year drought to fall on Israel because of the great sin of the king and his people. Angry, the king wanted Elijah to die and he would stop at nothing to find him. But God knew! God came alongside Elijah and instructed him to hide himself by the brook and that He would provide for his needs.

We don't know much about Elijah's time of isolation, his time at the brook Cherith – its very name speaking of separation. But we do know that God directed this time of hiding him away and providing for him. We know he was hidden at the brook for a year or more before God redirected him to take refuge with a widow and her son.

As this place of isolation presented before Elijah, he had two options – just as we have two options: follow God's wisdom and direction to rest at the brook, or to fight against this uncomfortable place. Rest and wait, or struggle against what is not to our liking while risking both our life and God's plan for our life. Do we sit and wait at the brook with anticipation of what is to come? Or do we step out and try to "fix it" in our own strength?

Often a time of separation is a time of squeezing out that which is "all about us," a time of yielding to God's plan instead of ours. This time opens our ears and eyes to the voice and direction of God.

His very presence becomes palpable in our lives, allowing our lives to become fruitful for His Kingdom.

Summary thought:

Realizing that God has hidden you by the brook, that He knows where you are, how you feel and exactly what you need is the FIRST step to finding hope in the middle of a hopeless time. Let's rest and wait at the brook, allowing God to reset our lives to His purposes.

Matt. 11:28 Come to me, all who labor and are heavy laden, and I will give you rest.

Isa. 40:31 but they who wait for the Lord shall renew their strength; they shall mount up with wings like eagles; they shall run and not be weary; they shall walk and not faint.

Ps. 62:5 For God alone, O my soul, wait in silence, for my hope is from him.

Personal Insights:
_____
_____
_____
_____
_____
_____

H: How Does this Apply to Me?
_____
_____
_____
_____

O: Observations:
_____
_____
_____
_____

P: Personal Prayer:
_____
_____
_____
_____

E: Expression Through My Life (Action Step):
_____
_____
_____
_____

The Widows Help

The brook was drying up, as month after month marched on without rain – giving way to a full year. Elijah knew God's promise to meet his needs had been fulfilled – and would perpetually be – as he continued to wait, listening for His voice. He knew God's direction would come at the right time. He stayed where God had placed him and trusted in that promise.

The morning seemed to start like every other morning for the past year, but this day would be different. The voice of God spoke and the time of waiting at the brook was being shifted. God spoke and directed Elijah to go into Zarephath and stay with a widow.

He took water and began his long, arduous journey. This trek would require endurance filled with eighty-five miles being traversed in the middle of a drought while still continuing to stay vigilant for any of the king's men that were still out hunting him. Yet, he pushed toward Zarephath. Questions swirled as he trudged, mile after mile, toward the unknown. But every day, as he grew closer to his destination, he fought away those questions as he intently listened for more of God's plan.

He often wondered, "Who is this widow I am to meet? How will I know her? What if she chooses not to help me?"

All the unknown continued to swirl in the forefront of his mind, yet he knew God had sent him. And just as every other time he had heard Gods call, He would be faithful. So, he marched on toward what would come next for his life.

Upon entering the city after many days of traveling, he was hungry, thirsty and tired. He knew he was to meet a widow who would care for his needs, but who or where she was in this city would require eyes and ears on the alert and faith that God "had it all covered."

There, just as he entered the city gate, was a woman gathering sticks. Elijah requested water from her and a morsel of bread. Water she could get for him, but bread was a different matter. The drought had been bad, and she only had enough for one last meal for herself and her son before they would die from starvation.

His faith rose up within and he prophesied to her, "Go and make a cake for me first and then for yourself and son."

Just enough faith stirred within the widow as this "man of God" spoke to her, and she did as he requested. God responded and provided by filling her jar to overflowing with flour and oil. Because she had believed and done as requested, all three of them were provided for – not just for the day, but for the rest of the drought. Those jars of flour and oil continued to be filled to overflowing to meet their needs.

Staying with the widow, Elijah continued to wait, still hidden from the danger that was lurking as the three-year drought raged throughout the nation. This time he was hidden with others, this time learning new lessons to prepare him for what was still to come.

(Enjoy reading the whole story in 1 Kings 17:8-16)

This part of Elijah's story affected three people that God had plans for taking care of: Elijah, the widow and her son. Elijah chose to trust God to show him the right widow who God had planned to provide for him. He also believed that what God had spoken would come to pass. The widow, in a hopeless place, was given a choice – a possible lifeline for her and her son – but that choice required her to extend hospitality to a stranger, as well as believing this was a "man of God" who *just might* be there to help her.

This new place of hiding for Elijah was a new place of humbling. He now was staying in the home of an unknown widow and her son and he was dependent on her hospitality and provision. God made sure all was provided for, but this was another time of learning, growing and stepping out in faith as the prophet of God waited patiently for God's call and direction. During his time with the widow he was physically strengthened for what was to come.

For the widow, her choice to help him was her "last ditch" effort to possibly save herself and her son in the midst of this devastating famine. She was at a completely hopeless crossroad in her life when Elijah, a man of faith, filled with hope and promise, stepped before her asking for her help. She saw something she needed – hope – and she said, "Yes."

When we are placed into a time of "sheltering in place" or "isolation," whether it be for our safety, due to political and social unrest, due to an illness, a job change, or for any other reason, we are often not in it alone. We take others into that place with us. Our response and choices directly affect them. Do we encourage and bring them a lifeline of hope? Or do we draw them into our own place of despair?

Summary thought:

Understanding that Christ is your anchor, your salvation and your hope in all situations, allows you to be the one who can walk through life-altering changes with faith that will both draw the lost and hurting, as well as give hope to those around you. We are called to a great purpose – one of bringing hope to the hopeless!

Heb. 10:23 Let us hold fast the confession of our hope without wavering, for he who promised is faithful.

Ps. 39:7 And now, God, I'm left with one conclusion: my only hope is to hope in you alone! (TPT)

Rom. 12:12 Let this hope burst forth within you, releasing a continual joy. Don't give up in a time of trouble, but commune with God at all times. (TPT)

Personal Insights:
_____
_____
_____
_____
_____
_____

H: How Does this Apply to Me?
_____
_____
_____
_____

O: Observations:
_____
_____
_____
_____

P: Personal Prayer:
_____
_____
_____
_____

E: Expression Through My Life (Action Step):
_____
_____
_____
_____

Consuming Fire

*L*ife moved along as Elijah knit into the small family of the widow and her son. He continued to wait for Gods appointed time to be fulfilled. Two more years passed as the drought raged on all around him. And at the completion of three years of drought, the voice of God whispered again.

It was time. This devastating environmental disaster was soon to end, but it would require him to return and confront the king. God had sheltered, provided, strengthened and encouraged him, preparing him for this time. He would now need to stand before the very king who had diligently searched for him and declared to have him killed.

He presented himself before the king and boldly spoke, "I have not troubled Israel, but you have, and your father's house, because you have abandoned the commandments of the Lord and followed the Baals."

This was why he had been protected and prepared: to stand and declare that his God was the only God and Lord of Israel. He would not only declare this before the king, but before the nation. The decision that the nation would be required to make was who would they serve – God or Baal – no longer waffling between two gods.

In faith Elijah knew that Israel had to SEE the power of his God – the only true God. He presented to the king a test between his God and the king's god, Baal. The test would determine who would respond and prove himself to be the true, powerful one. He told the King to call all his prophets – those who stood for Baal – and have them prepare a sacrifice.

Elijah was willing to wait and watch as they asked Baal to come and consume it. The crowd of Baal prophets prepared their sacrifice and surrounded it with cries, pleas and even physical cutting of their bodies as they expected Baal to send fire down to consume their sacrifice, proving that he was a god to be worshiped. Hours marched on as this performance continued, but no answer was received.

Righteous indignation rose up in Elijah and he couldn't help but taunt them, "Cry aloud, for he is a god. Either he is musing, or relieving himself, or he is on a journey, or perhaps he is asleep and must be awakened"
(1 Kings 18:27). There was no answer.

It was then his turn to stand up for his God. Elijah knew God and that His plan and purpose was to turn His people back to Him. This was the time God had directed him to – a time for God's presence and power to be shown. He prepared an offering, built a stone alter, dug a trench around it, laid out the offering and then saturated it with water until the trench was full. Then in one faith-filled statement he called out to God to show Himself to be the only God, the God of Israel.

Elijah declared, "Oh Lord, God of Abraham, Isaac, and Israel, let it be known this day that you are God in Israel, and that I am your servant, and that I have done all these things at your word. Answer me, O Lord, answer me, that this people may know that you O Lord, are God, and that you have turned their hearts back" (1 Kings 18: 36-37).

In an instant the power of exploding fire consumed not only the offering, but also all the water and stone, leaving only dry ground. The people were in awe as their hearts were turned back to the one and only true God of Israel.

This was the purpose of these three years of drought and famine. This was the purpose God had called him to. This was why he had been hidden these last three years: to bring God's people to their knees in repentance.

The rain would now be released by God's merciful hand. The drought would end and the healing of His nation would begin. God's purpose was completed as Elijah was obedient to the voice of his Lord.

(Enjoy reading the whole story in 1 Kings 18)

Trust is built within us as we push through the waiting. As children at Christmas time, we learn early how hard it is to wait as we watch packages arrive – even shaking, touching and imagining what might be inside waiting for us. But, wait we must, for that time of opening is set on a calendar. We wait for the perfectly ordained time for that gift to be received.

We continue to learn this waiting process throughout our lives – waiting to graduate into the unknown life ahead, waiting as wedding preparation comes to fruition, waiting nine months for the delivery of a child. And then there are the monumental times where waiting is beyond our strength to endure. Waiting to come out of the darkness as we persevere through an illness, through joblessness or even through destructive relationships. These are the times where survival is somewhat obscured as we drag through the seemingly useless, destructive waiting.

Waiting stinks! But waiting with anticipation will get us through to the other side as long as our mind is stayed on the presence, wisdom and direction of God.

You must fight forward with the understanding that even in the midst of the darkness, God has a plan – an assignment for your life that can only be produced as you surrender to the adjustments that take place here in the darkness.

Does He want you to suffer? Absolutely not! But does He know exactly where you are? YES! His ultimate goal in your life is to see you complete your life purpose, your heavenly assignment. We are just like Elijah. He was hidden during a dark time in history, and in this hidden place he was driven to a deeper personal relationship with God – one that was free from distractions.

Allow this time of waiting to drive you not into self-pity and frustration, but to the foot of the cross. Make room in this out-of-control, unknown, free-fall place to meet with Him daily, grow in His Word, hear His voice and listen for His plan for your next move. Expect to hear, grow and be adjusted into who He desires you to become. For His heart is to use you to touch others' lives, to give hope to the hopeless and to turn the hearts of the people back to worship the one and only – true God.

Summary thought:

Surrendering to the flow of life around you, in the midst of uncertainty, requires a deep faith and trust that God's plan for you is not over. He has ordained times and purposes! Our thoughts, strategies, desires and even needs are "man's ideas," not God's.

When you walk in faith with eyes on Christ and His assignment for you, allowing Him to adjust you through life's circumstances you will grow, be strengthened and – yes – you will be humbled along the way. However, leaning in with anticipation of the outcome for His glory will stir great hope within you, and joy will erupt in a life of fulfillment.

2 Cor. 5:7 for we walk by faith, not by sight.

Jer. 29:11 For I know the plans I have for you, declares the Lord, plans for welfare and not for evil, to give you a future and a hope.

Gal. 3:3 Are you so foolish? Having begun by the Spirit, are you now being perfected by the flesh?

Personal Insights:
_____
_____
_____
_____
_____

H: How Does this Apply to Me?
_____
_____
_____
_____

O: Observations:
_____
_____
_____
_____

P: Personal Prayer:
_____
_____
_____
_____

E: Expression Through My Life (Action Step):
_____
_____
_____
_____

Chapter 3

Hidden for an Eternal Plan

Heb. 5:9 And being made perfect, he became the source of eternal savation to all who obey him,

Hidden for an Eternal Plan

Stories from the Life of Jesus

The word "lockdown" immediately stirs negative and unwanted feelings and emotions. This word has recently come to the forefront of our society, but our experiences have quickly taught us that our life will be *restricted and limitations will ensue*.

From His conception to maturity and from maturity to His release into ministry, Jesus lived a life relatively under a *lockdown* that God established for His safety, instruction and ultimate glory. He was hidden within a willing and yielded mother and protected by an earthly father who created a place of refuge and training. Jesus was prepared for the greatest battle ever waged – a battle for our eternal souls.

The enemy's voice points us to restrictions, limitations and, "I can't," while the voice of God points us to freedom, safety and preparations that can only be found in the hidden places.

What we see as *negative*, is God's opportunity of *celebration*. You will find all that God has available for you – on the other side of *lockdown*.

Accepted Assignment

The arrival of an unexpected visitor changed the mundane daily tasks of her life forever. There was no question in her mind regarding who this visitor was; his radiant glow and powerful presence filled the whole house. However, the "why" hung heavy in the air as he declared, "Do not be afraid, Mary, for you have found favor with God. And behold, you will conceive in your womb and bear a son, and you shall call his name Jesus. He will be great and will be called the Son of the Most High" (Luke 1:30-32). She openly conversed with him regarding this possibility and quickly accepted with joy this divine assignment.

Young and inexperienced, her natural concerns and apprehensions stirred fear, "What will everyone say? How can I explain this? Will anyone believe me?"

The angel had told her of Elizabeth's pregnancy for a purpose and she wondered, "Did he know I would have worries and concerns? Did he tell me of Elizabeth to give me a place for support?" Her thoughts drove her to leave her home and travel to the hills in order to visit with Elizabeth.

What a relief – the Spirit of God had prepared Elizabeth to receive her. In an instant, God's Spirit had revealed the great gift to humanity that was growing in Mary's womb, so there was no need for her to try to explain. The explaining would have to be done in three months when she returned home. But, for now, she could rejoice in God's miracle growing within.

The whispered gossip upon her return was difficult, but God sent Joseph a dream to confirm that the child conceived within her was from the Holy Spirit. The plans for a quiet divorce were set aside as a hurried wedding was performed.

She relished in every kick and movement of life within her. She wondered, "What kind of mother will I be to this special child? What will he look like? Who will he become?" Deep inside, she knew she would need to trust God more than ever before.

Months passed, and daily life in Nazareth began to stir with the announcement that a census was to be declared; all the while, her baby grew bigger and stronger within her womb. Traveling to Bethlehem to register was not going to be fun. Her concerns weighed heavy on her mind as her baby weighed heavy in her body.

Traveling for miles, sometimes walking and sometimes riding, the hot desert sun gave her no respite. This journey was the most difficult part of Mary's pregnancy. As contractions began, she knew that what had been difficult all day was about to end with her infant in her arms – but how and where was her immediate concern.

Arriving in Bethlehem should have brought her relief – but as the pain seared through her body, and inn after inn had no place for them, it became obvious that they had to stop somewhere before this baby was delivered in the street. With great relief, a stable was provided for them; though this was not her plan for delivery, it was God's – for it had been prophesied that His son would come into the world as a humble servant. And that is how he arrived – wrapped and lying in a manger.

Remarkable announcements were made in the heavens, and unexpected visitors arrived with adoration and gifts while Mary and Joseph marveled, "Who is this child that we have been entrusted with?" All of these events were stored up within the hearts of Mary and Joseph as they rejoiced in his arrival. They would watch him grow and become the very Son of God.

(Enjoy reading the whole story in Luke 1-2)

There is something that occurs when we lay down our desires and say, "Yes, Lord," to His requests. It is an overwhelming, supernatural opportunity for the Holy Spirit to step into the room and overshadow our intentions with His. Then what is hidden inside of us will begin to grow and be strengthened. Inside our hidden places a maturing begins to occur, as what has been spoken waits patiently for its time to be birthed.

We won't be expecting to birth the Savior of the world, but there are gifts and talents within each of us that He desires to use, hone and ignite into new places where the world can see the glory of God revealed. It might be a new business, artistic endeavor, place of teaching, opportunity to encourage or so much more. If He has begun to stir something new inside of you – something way too big for you to accomplish on your own – listen closely, take a deep breath and trust Him.

Saying, "Yes, Lord," is never easy and always comes with a cost. Time and patience will begin to incubate within you as those words leave your lips.

Just as Mary spent nine months with Jesus growing within her, you will need to trust God in your own waiting process. It could be days, months or even years in the germinating, but do not give up. If He called you to it and you said yes, He will always faithfully work out the process in your life.

Living in a world that has become "instant" in every way, we have forgotten how to be patient and wait. With instant meals, continual live streaming of our favorite TV shows, fast food via 24-hr drive-ups and even free overnight delivery of anything we want; we have a hard time waiting for anything.

Plant a garden from seed next spring, and you will find yourself checking every day to see if you have Produce yet. The reality of the process is slow: seed (be it in the natural or the spiritual) must germinate, grow strong roots, produce the plant that will allow the flower to bloom; then comes pollination and finally the fruit begins. But sadly, you still must wait. The fruit now must be fed the right amount of nutrients, receive adequate water and sunshine and – finally – the long-anticipated produce triumphantly arrives.

Any time God begins to speak a vision, direction or idea into your heart, it will require faith to say yes. Mary was faced with the same questions we have, "Are you sure Lord? How will that happen? What will everyone say?" Once you say, "Yes, Lord! – Let it be so," it will require obedience and patience to stay the course.

The in-between process is important – it is in this place that you will find your faith tested. Temptation to give up will whisper, "It is just too hard," while our natural tendency to wave the white surrender flag is crouching on the chair right next to us. Here you must remember Mary. During her long, hot journey, giving up was not an option. She had been given an assignment – to carry the Savior of the world within her – and that would become the greatest treasure this world has ever received.

Stand firm in the call that has been spoken into you, step up and, with confidence, respond with an obedient, "Yes, Lord." Don't doubt, but patiently wait in the hidden place of preparation for its birth.

<u>Summary thought:</u>

Faith to believe in any call to action or acceptance of assignment from God must be responded to. How you answer will require a choice to step-out and say, "Yes, Lord," or to shake your head and ignore it. But I encourage you to say, "Yes, Lord," as He always has the best in mind for you.

In the midst of the process, allow His presence to hide you under His wings. Stay in that hidden place while the seed germinates and your roots grow, and wait patiently all the way to the time of harvest. During that time, you will develop a patient expectation of the birth to come.

Luke 8:15 As for that in the good soil, they are those who, hearing the word, hold it fast in an honest and good heart, and bear fruit with patience.

2 Cor. 1:20 For all of God's promises find their "yes" of fulfillment in him. And as his "yes" and our "amen" ascent to God, we bring him glory! (TPT)

Heb. 11:1 Now faith brings our hopes into reality and becomes the foundation needed to acquire the things we long for. It is all the evidence required to prove what is still unseen. (TPT)

Personal Insights:

_____
_____
_____
_____
_____
_____

H: How Does this Apply to Me?

_____
_____
_____
_____

O: Observations:

_____
_____
_____
_____

P: Personal Prayer:

_____
_____
_____
_____

E: Expression Through My Life (Action Step):

_____
_____
_____
_____

A Father's Refuge

*H*is eyes flew open and his heart pounded within his chest. The dream was not just any dream, but a warning carrying urgent instructions. He did not have time to question it, only to believe and move.

He had seen and heard too much since the conception and birth of his son to allow normal thoughts to stir. He quickly put the undercurrent of questions aside, as he immediately woke his wife. They gathered their belongings, prepared their son and rode away into the night.

Protection of Jesus was priority to both Joseph and God. Without questioning, Egypt became their destination and no return date was known. The days of travel where hot and dusty as plans of creating a new life in a foreign country were bantered back and forth between him and Mary.

Joseph's heart was heavy as he thought of the horror that was now taking place in Bethlehem and its surrounding regions. Herod had declared every child aged two years old and under to be killed. This dark cloud weighed formidably over him as he traveled toward Egypt, escaping the massacre. His primary focus was to protect the son entrusted to him and keep him hidden from the enemy's destruction.

Arriving in Egypt and starting a new life didn't last long. Before two years passed, Herod had died and God again directed Joseph to move – this time he would be headed back to Israel. However, he was gripped with fear along the way, as he heard that Herod's son was on the throne.

Being warned in a dream, he turned toward Galilee and settled in Nazareth instead.

The new life in Nazareth was good to Joseph and his family. He often thought of the years that had been filled with joy as he trained up his son in God's ways, while productively instructing him in his own trade of carpentry. Jesus had grown like anyone else – from infant to toddler, toddler to child and child to adolescent – nothing unusual. But the knowledge of who he would become was always quietly waiting to be revealed.

Joseph knew that the day of his son's purpose was soon to be revealed. He had seen the wisdom and favor of God upon him as Jesus matured.

Then, there was that day they had found him teaching in the temple. After their annual trip to the temple in Jerusalem, Jesus had stayed behind while the family began their travel toward home. Joseph found him missing and began the search. Several days were filled with anxious backtracking – only to find Jesus sitting contentedly, astounding the leaders of the temple with his wisdom.

Joseph knew his entrusted assignment – the place of parental refuge – would soon come to an end as Jesus stepped into his God-ordained, eternal purpose.

(Enjoy the whole story in Matt. 2:13-23)

If you are a believer in Jesus Christ, you know that He has a plan and purpose for everyone – yes, you too – right where you are, and even if it's in the midst of what may appear very bleak right now. As we see the chaos that surrounds us, it is easy to close the door, bury our heads in the sand and wait for it all to go away. Joseph could have done that – he could have just been content to raise this foster child and live his normal life.

BUT – God!!! God has a way of waking us up – speaking simply (sometimes in a whisper, sometimes with a shout) to move us. He may use a dream like He did with Joseph, He may use the Word of God or He may use a spoken Word from a trusted pastor. But when He does and when we hear, we must respond in an instant. Joseph's quick response to God's direction saved the life of Jesus. God's direction to us today can be just as life-impacting.

If we are lethargic in our response, allowing doubt or even our own control and opinions to be mulled around in our thoughts, we may end up where we don't want to be; our very lives or our families could be in jeopardy.

Finding ourselves today in a necessary, isolated society, our ears must stay tuned to the voice of God, not man. Opinions run rampant all around, but it is the voice of God where we find truth. Our instant response, without wavering, must be like Joseph's. God told him to move for the safety of His son, and not just once. God's instruction got him to Egypt, out of the grasp of Herod's destructive rampage – but also, upon his return, brought him into Nazareth to grow under Joseph's fatherly instruction.

Joseph accepted willingly his assignment – to protect, care and raise God's son. He chose to make a refuge for Jesus where he would mature and flourish. And throughout that thirty years, Joseph gave up his own control over his life and trusted God's control.

The key we must stand on during this time of our own societal hiding is one of willingness to let our own thoughts and opinions go and trust in God's control. Ultimately, our trust must find its hope in God alone. Our refuge must be found not in man's ways and opinions, but at the foot of the Cross. Our safety and security are not found in a political party or its leader – it is found in the King of kings, whose throne reigns with authority over all.

So, rest assured in His plan and His purpose for your life. He is not finished with you – He has a divine, eternal assignment for you. Listen with ears tuned to His voice and, just as Joseph watched and waited for Jesus to step into His divine purpose, watch and wait for His direction in yours.

<u>Summary thought:</u>

Take time away from the fray of society's input to tune your ears to the voice of God and be willing to respond to His direction. Allow Him to transform your thoughts and opinions, lining them up with His Word, His voice and His plan for your life. Be willing to step out as He directs you. Be willing to move into His ordained purpose for your life. And be willing to become a refuge of support – an encourager to others – and the living example of the love of Christ to those around you.

Rom. 12:2 Stop imitating the ideals and opinions of the culture around you, but be inwardly transformed by the Holy Spirit through a total reformation of how you think. This will empower you to discern God's will as you live a beautiful life, satisfying and perfect in his eyes. (TPT)

James 1:19 Know this, my beloved brother: let every person be quick to hear, slow to speak, slow to anger;

1 Thess. 2:4 but just as we have been approved by God to be entrusted with the gospel, so we speak not to please man, but to please God who tests our hearts,

Personal Insights:
___
___
___
___
___
___
___

H: How Does this Apply to Me?
___
___
___
___

O: Observations:
___
___
___
___

P: Personal Prayer:
___
___
___
___

E: Expression Through My Life (Action Step):
___
___
___
___

Wilderness Preparation

The Father's approval rang out over him as he rose from the waters of baptism. The multitude of people pressed in from the shore. They were in awe as a dove descended on this man, and the voice of God rumbled over their heads. Whispers and declarations joined together with one single question, "Who is this man?"

With the Holy Spirit's arrival, in the form of a dove, God confirmed to Jesus that the ministry He was ordained to fulfill was about to begin. His first task was to overcome the tempting tactics of Satan and, as He was directed, He marched into the wilderness ready for the confrontation.

As He journeyed into the desert, away from city life, a deep stillness grew within Him. Out in the desert, nothing distracted Him; His focus was set on the presence of His Father. A time of prayer and fasting would settle everything into a single focus: a single focus that He knew would be required. Jesus knew this time in the wilderness was necessary, and that it would strengthen and prepare Him for God's divine plan.

Several days passed as heat, thirst, hunger and lack of adequate rest began to affect Him. He pressed in closer to His Father, to the scriptures He knew well and to the voice He listened intently for – the voice of wisdom and encouragement.

As night began to close in around Him, He watched as a small animal scurried across the desert floor, not far from where He sat. A low growl whispered off to His right, and in an instant a powerful lunge was followed by the crunching of bones. The weaker animal had succumbed to the attack of the stronger.

When morning arrived, He continued to contemplate the night's lesson. The enemy that He was here to vanquish was also waiting just like a wild animal, waiting to attack and devour its prey – and he was that prey. But He knew the outcome! He knew this confrontation must come and that He would battle to overcome. The battle was about to begin as His physical body weakened.

His stomach rumbled with need as a whisper began to be heard. Satan stepped up and, just like the low growl of an animal ready to attack its prey, he began to taunt who Jesus was, "If you are the Son of God, command this stone to become bread" (Luke 4:3). This did little to distract Jesus from the battle, for He knew who He was. He could easily have turned the stone to bread, but He knew God's plan. With confidence, He quickly responded, "It is written, 'Man shall not live by bread alone'" (Luke 4:4).

The battle raged on as Satan tried different tactics, including the use of scripture, in order to manipulate Jesus into his trap of destruction. The devil knew who Jesus was and thought he had the perfect attack mechanism as he took him high up to see the splendor and greatness that surrounded Him. Satan offered Jesus all the glory and authority that he controlled – all He would need to do was worship him and it was all His.

The Father's approval had sealed within Jesus the "who" of who He was. He knew, as the Son of God, He already had all glory and authority in the heavens – this satanic strategy would not work. He responded, "It is written, 'You shall worship the Lord your God, and Him only shall you serve'" (Luke 4:8)

Each skirmish came with different barbs of attack as the devil battled on, bringing one temptation after another, but each met defeat. As days of temptation continued, the whispers and shouts from Satan were overcome as Jesus prayed, walked in the presence of his Father, leaned on the words of scripture and was ministered to by Heaven's angelic forces.

This last morning, Jesus was swept up to the pinnacle of Jerusalem's temple, and with one last taunt the devil said, "If you are the son of God, throw yourself down from here, for it is written, ' He will command his angels concerning you, to guard you,' and, 'On their hands they will bear you up, lest you strike your foot against a stone'" (Luke 4:9-11). With determination, Jesus simply responded, "It is said, 'You shall not put the Lord your God to the test'"
(Luke 4:12).

He knew this time of preparation and its victory was complete as He made His way home. But He also knew that this vicious predator was still waiting, lurking and ready to step back in at any moment to try a few more tactics in order to destroy Him and God's eternal plan. But for now, He had a great assignment to walk into, as He began declaring the Kingdom of God on earth and God's eternal plan for mankind. An assignment that would end at the Cross with the competed victory over this adversary.

(Enjoy reading the whole story in Luke 4:1-15)

Jesus walked into the wilderness, ready for a battle with the same adversary that we must also confront daily in our lives. How did He handle that coming fight? He went into it saturated with prayer and fasting; that's our example and, at some point, you will also need to elicit these two practices.

The temptation that Jesus underwent was a direct combat and victory that occurred between heaven and hell, in a place of divine preparation that was found in the desert wilderness – His place of isolation. Here, Jesus was tempted, and He overcame three of the devil's greatest lies. And this time was prefaced by a personal preparation of prayer and fasting. His battle, just like ours, begins in prayer – not a begging time, but a declaring time of warfare and of battle that still must take place between heaven and hell.

Hidden away in the wilderness, for forty days, Jesus chose to fast and pray as He prepared for the battle that He would wage on our behalf. The battle began as preparation for the ministry He was to embark on; but if we look closer, it was the also the first battle fought on our behalf.

If you find yourself swirling in chaotic circumstances that seem to be pulling you under, now is the time to choose to step away into a time of personal hiding. A time of prayer and fasting, where distractions can be limited and your focus on the presence of God will stir peace and confidence in the victory that has already been won for you.

Satan is a sly enemy, and he threw everything into the fray as he tempted Jesus. He began his attack when Jesus was weakened and his barrage continued rigorously. If he planned his attack on Jesus this way, then we need to be very aware that he will come at us in the same type of timing: when we are weakest.

Strategic attacks from the devil come at us every day. His three favorite fronts are the same now as they were in the wilderness for Jesus:
- lust of the body (physical satisfaction or *hedonism*),
- lust of the eyes (wealth and possessions or *materialism*)
- pride of life (love of self or *egoism*).

Each of these temptations can find themselves sliding into our lives, often unbeknownst to us. However, once we see them, a decision to root them out must be made and the battle fought. Sounds like a battle you just don't want to accept? That's true for all of us and, thankfully, it has already been waged on our behalf – right out there in the wilderness and at the Cross of Christ. We just have to acknowledge it, lay it down at the Cross and walk away. I am not saying it will be easy – that is why it is called a battle and needs to be addressed with prayer and fasting. But to live a life full of God's planned abundance – this is where the *rubber meets the road*.

The victory that Jesus won out in the wilderness was also won for us. He was weak, just like you may be right now, yet He raised up a sword found in the Word and battled these lies of temptation by standing on the Word of God. Not flinching, He declared that He would not tempt, worship nor serve anyone but His God, nor would He live only to feed His body.

If you find yourself weak and going under: remember, so was Jesus. Find hope today in that He fought the same battles – the same temptations – and remember, you've *got this* because you are not alone.

Pull out your two greatest weapons – prayer and fasting – and fight forward, knowing you have a warrior that has already won this same fight before you and that He is in your corner cheering you on.

<u>Summary thought:</u>

Jesus' time in the wilderness was a time of preparation, ordained for victory, and was the beginning of God's eternal plan for all of mankind; it began with time set aside to pray and fast – to listen intently to the voice of His Father.

Our divine assignment will hold the same choice and the same temptations; choose to step into a place and time that is set aside to intently listen to the voice of your Father, to pray and fast and to fight back against the lies of Satan.

These two disciplines – prayer and fasting – are foundational in our Christian lifestyle. They are primary keys to living victoriously – pick up your weapons and fight forward.

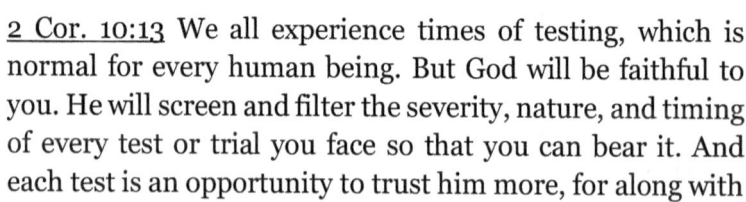

<u>2 Cor. 10:13</u> We all experience times of testing, which is normal for every human being. But God will be faithful to you. He will screen and filter the severity, nature, and timing of every test or trial you face so that you can bear it. And each test is an opportunity to trust him more, for along with every trial God has provided for you a way of escape that will bring you out of it victoriously. (TPT)

1 John 5:4 You see, every child of God overcomes the world, for our faith is the victorious power that triumphs over the world. (TPT)

Ps. 86:6 Give ear, O Lord, to my prayer; listen to my plea for grace.

Personal Insights:
_____
_____
_____
_____
_____
_____

H: How Does this Apply to Me?
_____
_____
_____
_____

O: Observations:
_____
_____
_____
_____

P: Personal Prayer:
_____
_____
_____
_____

E: Expression Through My Life (Action Step):
_____
_____
_____
_____

Chapter 4

Hidden to Preserve Life

J. K. Sanchez

Jer. 29:11 For I know the plans I have for you, declares the Lord, plans for welfare and not for evil, to give you a future and a hope.

Hidden to Preserve Life

Stories from the Life of Joseph

Our lives are permeated with opportunities for unforgiveness to take root and embitter our lives, changing us and those around us. Offense is always the underlying culprit. In this place, the enemy of our souls – the devil and his nasty cohorts – will slide right in under the radar. His purpose: divide and conquer. He wants us isolated and separated from any type of "togetherness." His goal is to cause suspicion, finger pointing and judgment, all while he is driving a divisive barb deep into our heart.

What does this thought have to do with the Bible story of Joseph? A lot!

A God-given dream to a very young man, fueled with a side-of-pride, began the offense which then allowed anger and judgment to grow, and led to murderous intent that would be implemented by his own brothers.

From the bottom of an abandoned well, bound and sent into slavery in Egypt, captivated in the King's Prison, and then all the way to the Pharaoh's Court – Joseph lived with God's favor over his life to preserve life for a nation. What the enemy thought would destroy him and his purpose, instead allowed a life that was hidden away from his family, ultimately preparing him for God's planned endgame, both for the nation and his life.

The Bottom of a Well

*P*hysical, mental and emotional exhaustion circled him like a vulture as the heat intensely radiated over him. He had been marching for days in this caravan, and he knew his fate looked bleak. His emotional state moved from sadness to anger, not understanding the "why" for the betrayal that landed him here.

As the sleepless nights in the quiet of the desert gave him time to consider this turn of events, he grappled to understand how this could have happened to him. He remembered the night when he had tossed and turned as the second dream from God had stirred within him. Visions of both dreams now vividly played out in his mind – the bending sheaves and then the bowing down of the sun, moon and stars. These dreams had circled in his thoughts as morning arrived. "Wow, that dream confirmed the first. I can't wait to tell my family," he had thought.

"Maybe that was my first mistake. Maybe I should never have told them," he mused. Continuing to search for an answer, his mind spun in circles remembering how he had shared the first dream with his brothers and his surprise when it was met with ridicule. How he had thought that surely, once he shared the second dream, they would believe it and receive it as from God. He even made sure to share that one when his father was present. He knew his father's love and continual encouragement should have been an influence on his brothers – that they would hear the "truth" behind those dreams. But when he shared the *second dream, even his father questioned it. He knew he was his father's favorite son – but, unfortunately, he now could see that all his older brothers knew it, too. "Maybe I offended them and was too prideful in my announcing both the favor of my father and of God's dreams," he concluded.*

The story Joseph didn't know, as he continued to process his current situation and the circumstances that had landed him here in the middle of the desert, would bring life-long impact to his brothers and father.

The undercurrent of offense was often spoke of between his brothers, "How could Joseph think that he would be so grand that we would bow to him and that even our parents would bow down before him?"

Betrayal was close on the heels of offense as the opportunity for judgement arrived. His brothers were out caring for the flocks when his father requested that Joseph go out and check on them.

His brothers saw Joseph coming in the distance. Seeing him approaching in his beautiful coat that their father made for him – and only him – brought antagonistic thoughts to them. "Here comes the dreamer. We just need to get rid of him. Toss him into the well," they discussed.

When Joseph arrived and questioned his brothers as to what they had been doing, the tense climate between them came to a head. Before Joseph knew it, he was grabbed; his coat was ripped from his shoulders and he was thrown down the deep, dry well. He landed with a thud as the dust rose all around him. He shouted, pleaded and begged them to pull him out. But all his commotion seemed to have no effect on the brothers. But as the brothers sat resting and sharing a midday meal, a caravan headed to Egypt came along and a more devious plot emerged.

"Let's sell him and get something for him. Our hands won't be covered by his blood this way. We can take his coat back to Father, and he will believe that he was eaten by wild animals," they schemed and plotted. They didn't care about the pain that shot through Joseph as he hit the floor of the well or the mental confusion they just inflicted on their little brother. His cries of, "What is going on? What have I done? Why are you, my own brothers treating me this way?" went unanswered. Ultimately, they decided on Joseph's fate; they pulled him up from the bottom of the well, bound his hands and sold him off into slavery.

Joseph put aside his musings when the arrival of his coming fate materialized upon entering Egypt. Its busy, chaotic sounds and smells sent fear into his heart. His thoughts of, "Why?" and his desperate pleading with his brothers for freedom were quickly replaced with, "What now?" and, "Oh God, please help me – I am your servant."

He was roughly pushed forward as bidding for his life began. It didn't take long – suddenly he heard, "Sold!" He was now a slave, and his life would take a new direction, one that, unknown to Joseph, would ultimately prepare and place him in the exact place that God had ordained.

(Enjoy reading the whole story in Gen. 37: 1-36)

The overwhelming feelings that Joseph experienced are no different than when betrayal and unexpected life changes enter our own lives. Have you ever been there, or are you there now? Most of us have been or will be. Some of us will find ourselves there many times during our lives.

Satan's tactic of division always brings with it a deep seat of judgement. "I am right, and they are wrong," rings through our hearts and minds; once we open ourselves to that thinking, the enemy wins. Our hearts quickly assimilate to a place of suspicion and finger pointing. The final nail becomes a bitter, unforgiving, judgmental barb that is difficult to overcome. Unchecked, it will drive you into places that can affect your life and those around you for a lifetime.

Why is it so easy for us to quickly slip into this place? Simply put: it's pride! We all fall prey to this negative attribute. At only seventeen, Joseph did; announcing not once, but twice, the dreams that God gave him – dreams that clearly were understood to place him in a position over his brothers. All his brothers fell victim to this insidious monster, too, thinking that they were better than Joseph and deserved what their father didn't give them. The story may have had a different outcome on all of them if that barb of pride hadn't been interjected.

Pride, judgement and betrayal always go hand-in-hand to the bottom of a hidden, ugly, dark well. When you find yourself there, you can either feed it or realize your error and humbly cry out for the hand of Christ to pull you out. This place of repentance is the only place where you can break off what the enemy thought he could use to destroy you.

The forgiveness of Jesus and His unlimited grace is always waiting to free you from the well. However, consequences may still need to be paid by you and those around you.

God uses the circumstances that we find ourselves in to prepare us for His plans and purposes – even those brought on by our own pride or the judgments and betrayals of others. Some of those preparations will require times of separation, times of difficult life change or times when you cry out, "I don't want to do this anymore!" But when you keep your face looking up to Jesus from the bottom of that well, you will find His favor and love waiting for you.

Remember you are not alone. Keep your eyes on Christ. Remember that Jesus paid for a very special place for you in eternity. And remember that He has a planned purpose for you to accomplish right here on earth. Know that what the enemy planned for harm in your life can be turned into gold when you humble yourself before the hand of God.

Summary thought:

We hear the truth in the well-known statement, "United we stand, divided we fall," but we easily relinquish that truth for the enemy's lie of, "I am right, and they are wrong." When we let go of the pride that separates us, we will find that the love of Jesus will reign in our lives.

Don't allow judgement, pride or betrayal to keep you buried at the bottom of the well – trust the favor and restoration of Christ to move your life forward into new places of success.

1 Pet. 5:6 If you bow low in God's awesome presence, he will eventually exalt you as you leave the timing in his hands. (TPT)

James 4:12 There is only one lawgiver and judge, he who is able to save and to destroy. But who are you to judge your neighbor?

Rom. 15:7 You will bring God glory when you accept and welcome one another as partners, just as the Anointed One has fully accepted you and received you as his partner. (TPT)

Personal Insights:
_____
_____
_____
_____
_____
_____

H: How Does this Apply to Me?
_____
_____
_____
_____

O: Observations:
_____
_____
_____
_____

P: Personal Prayer:
_____
_____
_____
_____

E: Expression Through My Life (Action Step):
_____
_____
_____
_____

Favor Meets False Accusation

*T**he favor of God quickly began to be seen on Joseph as he settled into his new life in the service of the officer of the pharaoh. God's presence and blessing surrounded Joseph as he accepted this life as a slave. Early on it became apparent to Potiphar that Joseph was a man of integrity, knowledge and wisdom. His abilities to lead became a great asset to everything that he set his hands to, and soon Potiphar no longer needed to manage the minuscule details of the running of his house – they all fell to the capable hands of his new slave, Joseph.*

This new life was not so bad; he had been very blessed to end up here. Settling into the flow of everyday life was easy – he had always excelled at managing details, and God was faithful to continue giving him wisdom, even here in this foreign and unusual culture. All that he directed had success, and Potiphar continued to add more responsibility for him to carry; soon he was in charge of everything.

He grew stronger – no longer a child – and with that his success grew. However, along with success, the eye of Potiphar's wife was drawn to him. He found no problem being daily in the house with her; she was the wife of his owner and the only thing that was "off limits." No temptation stirred in him – he knew that any thought toward her would be sinful to his God and a sure death sentence from his owner.

On what would be his last morning at Potiphar's home, the breeze came through the window while he worked and brought a much-needed refreshing of the air that had been stifling for months. His mind drifted slightly as he contemplated the last few anxious days.

He had been staving off the unwanted attention that Potiphar's wife continued to flaunt at him. He had kept his mind and actions busy, attending to all that he oversaw, all the while feeling her growing frustration at his "slights" to her attention. He was faithful to his owner in every area and stepping over that line was not a place he would go. He never imagined what would transpire by the end of the day.

As he passed her in the hall, she sidled up close, asking, tempting and again presenting an offer she expected him to fulfill. This time his adamant refusal to her suggestion was too much for her to handle. In frustration, she reached out and grabbed at his garment as he bolted away from her.

Indignation and anger quickly turned to an opportunity for revenge – she shouted for the guards, playing the victim of an attempt of seduction from her husband's trusted overseer, Joseph. As soon as her husband arrived home, the rouse continued as she produced the torn garment retrieved from her bed. An angry declaration from her husband quickly followed, and Joseph was taken prisoner.

For the second time in his short life, Joseph found himself grabbed and thrown into a dark life-changing place. This time False Accusation joined with Betrayal to place him where they agreed to destroy and hide him away for good. He would be isolated in the King's Prison for years – hidden, but not yet forgotten.

(Enjoy reading the whole story in Gen. 39:1-20)

False accusation always comes unexpectedly and often from someone who you have called a friend. These lies are the deepest form of betrayal, and the cut severely perforates your heart. If you have been there, you know the bitter, shattered door that opens before you. The floor drops out, the walls press in and the ceiling threatens to crush you. You have no control, you have no defense and you have no hope.

When falsely accused, your character is always called into question. This tactic of Satan is used to undermine and destroy. For Joseph, he had fought the temptation, ran from it and had not succumbed to its seduction. But the accusation appeared to be correct to all those around him. He was given no audience, he had no defense and the judgement gavel rattled as the prison doors slammed shut. Have you ever been there? The indignation and shock clambers loudly in your head, "How could they believe that?" Well, if you have ever been in or are in this devastating place now, remember you are in good company.

Joseph found himself, for the second time, isolated from what his normal life had been. He had the same choices that we do when we are faced with falsehoods: wallow in the "poor me" attitude, buying into despair and self-pity, or to trust God's steadfast love.

How you ultimately respond to these life-altering betrayals is where the devil sits, waiting to pounce. The door has been cracked opened – the unfairness easily drives you to frustration and anger as thoughts of revenge creep into your heart. The crack slowly widens into a gap – the hurt and pain push you into hopelessness and despair. Now he dives in for the kill, as the door is wide open – pride rises up to take control and hammer bitterness deep into your heart.

There it will grow and allow destruction to walk through the door unchecked.

The key to slamming that door shut is found hidden at the foot of the Cross. Our willingness to humbly give up our "rightness" requires a broken and empty self. All control has to be poured out before Him in prayer – cry it out, shout it out – He already knows the pain you are in. Here you can lay it down – all down. Here you will find the strength to stand up again, slam that door and move forward into God's new direction for your life.

The pain does not go away in an instant; the unfairness will raise its head often. But, every time, a choice must be made to push back, and once again, close that door. Knowing who you are in Christ is paramount in these times. Joseph knew God, trusted that He had a plan for him and found God's favor as he continued to walk in the integrity of his character – even in the darkness of prison.

When you walk in integrity, light and favor will direct your path. A path that will lead you into God's preparation. The path toward His plan and purpose for your life is usually much different than yours. It will require a road that does not promise a smooth downhill grade, but one that is full of rocks, mountains and even a few toppled trees along the way.

Sitting down and giving up is not an option; giving God the control and trusting Him in the process will allow Him to dig deep within you, realigning you to become who God created you to be – a highly-favored child of the King who has a specific assignment from the throne room – just as Joseph did.

Summary thought:

Choose to walk through your life with integrity, even when lies swirl around you, pain and injustice take your breath away and it seems like there is no hope. It is right there in that dark prison that the choice shouts out to be made, "Who will you believe – God's promise for abundant life, or the lies of man?

Choose today to get out of the prison, accept God's hand over your life, give up your control and trust that there is a light at the end of this tunnel.

Prov. 10:9 Whoever walks in integrity walks securely, but whoever takes crooked paths will be found out.

Ps. 51:17 The sacrifices of God are a broken spirit; a broken and contrite heart, O God, you will not despise.

Heb. 12:12-13 Therefore lift your drooping hands and strengthen your weak knees, and make straight paths for your feet, so that what is lame may not be put out of joint but rather be healed.

Personal Insights:
_____
_____
_____
_____
_____

H: How Does this Apply to Me?
_____
_____
_____

O: Observations:
_____
_____
_____

P: Personal Prayer:
_____
_____
_____

E: Expression Through My Life (Action Step):
_____
_____
_____

Prison's Isolation

*D*ay after day turned into months – then years – as he joined the monotony of life as a prisoner. He had wallowed in self-pity, anger and resentment for some time, as False Accusation and Betrayal cheered, but Joseph soon knew his only hope was to be found in his God. The steadfast love and favor of God again began to shine over his life, even in the depths of darkness that were found in the King's Prison.

His integrity and God's favor over his life and all that he touched was soon evident to the keeper of the prison. Joseph was placed in a position of leadership, even here in the darkness. He was put in charge of running the prison and all of its prisoners.

He befriended those around him – the guards and keeper, as well as the prisoners that lived alongside him. Often discussing questions of, "What brought you here?" it was not a surprise to find that False Accusation and Betrayal were part of every story. It wasn't his place to judge them, he just chose to listen.

Years passed with no justice or opportunity to prove his innocence. He remained faithful to his God and faithful to the position he found himself in. He trusted God, and God began to speak to him again through dreams and the interpretation of them.

Joseph was entrusted with the care of many of the king's officials, those who had fallen out of the king's favor and landed here, right along with him.

After a lengthy imprisonment, two servants of the king's kitchen staff came to him requesting his help. They were aware that God spoke to him, and they looked to him as a friend.

The night had been a long one as both the cupbearer and the baker dreamed, waking with unsettling questions. After discussing the oddity of their similar dreams, Joseph came to visit and found them confounded by the visions they had suffered in the night. He took this opportunity to declare his faith in God. Joseph said to them, "Do not all interpretations belong to God? Please tell them to me" (Genesis 40:8b).

He had become known for his ability to listen, his honesty and his caring. It wasn't new for prisoners to come requesting understanding of a dream, but this time the two standing before him had been in the court of the king. A stirring of hope rose with the possibilities, so he listened intently first to the men, then to the voice of God.

There is good and there is bad – and these two dreams presented both. He interpreted one dream of restoration to the cupbearer, and he asked to be remembered before the king when it was fulfilled. But to the baker, the interpretation was one of execution. Within three days they had been confirmed – one lifted back to his high position and the other one hung.

Anticipation grew in Joseph, as news and release of the cupbearer reached him. The promise to remember the interpretations he had shared quickly changed from ringing in his ears to yet one more pounding of betrayal, as months passed with no response, no request and no release.

(Enjoy the whole story in Gen. 39:21-23, 40:1-23)

Finding contentment in the midst of life adjustments is easier said than done. Trying to fix it, searching for strategies and mentally "spinning out" are all the normal responses to sudden change. No one likes it – in fact, we hate it – and do not want to accept it.

Joseph had to get through those same struggles, but soon he saw that he was not alone down there in the prison. He found others who he could encourage. He chose to be content where he found himself, kept his eyes on God and allowed Him to use him in the middle of the darkness. He became a listening friend to others, and God used him in the process.

Being used by God as an encourager comes from a heart that looks out for others. It is not about being set into a position, and it certainly doesn't happen because you "have it all together." One of the best places to speak life into others' lives is when you are at the bottom of your own; it is here that you can speak with humility. It won't be your words, because you barely have the strength to stand – it will be His words. And you will see life begin to bring them hope.

Joseph's imprisonment was a lengthy one. He was hidden away and submitted under God's hand of preparation for what is thought to be around ten years. Yet, in that place, he made the best of it. His integrity shined as he used his talents and gifts, rising to a leadership position again. God fine-tuned him in that darkness, weeding out any selfishness, left-over pride, or self-pity. He found God's faithful, steadfast love to be his place of refuge in that prison cell. God's hand of favor was made obvious to those around him – he became light in the darkness. It was in that hidden prison time that God continued his preparation for the leadership position that was to come.

Summary thought:

Do you find yourself hidden away, feeling forgotten and useless? Lift up your eyes to the keeper of your soul, know that His steadfast love surrounds you. You are not alone – look up from your deep pit and reach out to others to encourage them.

God is not finished with you – he is preparing you for His next planned assignment in your life.

Gen. 39:21 But the Lord was with Joseph and showed him steadfast love and gave him favor in the sight of the keeper of the prison.

Matt. 5: 14 "You are the light of the world. A city set on a hill cannot be hidden."

John 6:63 It is the Spirit who gives life; the flesh is no help at all. The words that I have spoken to you are spirit and life.

Personal Insights:
_____
_____
_____
_____
_____
_____

H: How Does this Apply to Me?
_____
_____
_____
_____

O: Observations:
_____
_____
_____
_____

P: Personal Prayer:
_____
_____
_____
_____

E: Expression Through My Life (Action Step):
_____
_____
_____
_____

Forgiveness and Restoration

Thirteen years since he had left his family; years of growth in his relationship and understanding of God and years of maturing into a man of integrity. Dark days of betrayal, anguish and false accusations had been graciously balanced by God's hand of favor and success wherever circumstances had landed him.

It had been two more years in the Kings Prison, waiting for a promised remembrance, when the day arrived – a summons from the pharaoh requesting his presence. He had been remembered, as no one could interpret the pharaoh's dreams; this must be the God-planned opportunity for freedom that he had been so long awaiting.

In anticipation, he considered that this was it – the time that his thirteen years of isolation had come to – the time of God's favor and freedom.

That morning Joseph boldly declared the meaning of the pharaoh's dreams: seven years of great plenty, followed by seven years of famine. With God's wisdom, he detailed what should be done and recommended that a wise overseer be appointed to complete the instructions. The pharaoh was greatly pleased and quickly determined, "Can we find a man like this, in whom is the Spirit of God? Since God has shown you all this, there is none so discerning and wise as you are. You shall be over my house, and all my people shall order themselves as you command" (Genesis 41:38-39).

Years swiftly passed as Joseph stepped into this place of honor, delegation and great favor in the land of Egypt.

As God directed, he prepared for the great famine that was to come. He prepared the land and would be ready to pour out the overflowing storehouses when the time of famine came. And the time did come – the great lack and cry of the people rose up – and because of the obedience of Joseph, the people would survive.

Day after day, he sat as governor, selling and distributing grain to those who came before him. But this day would be different. This day would surprise him, bringing up a deep-seated hurt – the betrayal that had set his life in a trajectory toward Egypt.

The famine had been great in Egypt and even harder on those far out into the desert areas. The small group of dirty, tired and hungry men stood before the only man that could help provide food for them and their families. They had made the long journey, hoping for help to survive; now bowing with respect before this unknown man.

He was unrecognizable to them, but Joseph knew who bowed before him: the very brothers who had betrayed him and sold him into slavery twenty-two years ago. The emotions stirred within him – how was he to respond? With wisdom, he questioned them, finding out that his father and youngest brother were still alive and well. He tested them, detained them and gave them a way to prove themselves men of changed integrity. And then provided the much-needed grain at no cost.

His heart was overwhelmed with forgiveness as he overheard their discussions of regret and anguish over what they had done to their brother, still not aware of who it was that stood before them.

Joseph sent them home, and for several months, one brother remained in custody waiting for his brothers to return with their youngest brother for the exchange.

As Joseph awaited their return, God continued a work of forgiveness in his heart.

The return with Benjamin, his youngest brother, brought great joy to Joseph, but he devised one more test. However, the emotional response and petition of mercy from his brothers gave way to a flood of forgiveness within him, and he revealed who he was. A heavy silence settled over the room as great fear and anguish swirled in each brothers' thoughts. But Joseph had already broken off the chains of betrayal that had haunted him for years and had chosen to forgive them.

He compassionately announced, "Do not be distressed because you sold me here, for God sent me before you to preserve life" (Genesis 45:5). The forgiveness and restoration between Joseph and his family allowed for years of abundant provision.

The planned purpose of the hand of God's preparation on a broken, prideful, betrayed young man prevailed. A young man who had submitted himself before God and in faith trusted as he waited for God's answer. The very survival of multitudes of people, including the Hebrew nation, was accomplished through a life hidden in obscurity – a man hidden in order to preserve life.

(Enjoy reading the whole story in Gen 41-47:1-12)

As our life stretches before us, we are oblivious of what it will hold. The wonderful surprises send us to the heights of joy, while the devastating losses find us lower than we ever think we can recover from – yet there is God, always there in the midst. We walk in joy and tears – a seemingly diametrically-opposed paradigm – yet in that space between, we find, grow and learn how to live a life of abundance.

The keys to this life of abundance are found in the process. They are found in the dark hidden places. The places where tears flow, where anger and frustration rage, where the despair of hopelessness overtakes us. But it is right there where we find the refuge, our only place to run – into the arms of Jesus. In the process we find His love and forgiveness. That key – the love and forgiveness of Jesus – will release us from prison. It will allow us to walk into a new life – a promised eternal life. The process still must have its way within us, but now we can say, "Yes, Lord." Submitting under His loving hand will allow us to find another crucial key: forgiveness. This time forgiveness of others.

Joseph learned this process of forgiveness, too. He walked through it as he was confronted with his brothers standing before him, needing his help. What he would choose – to forgive or get revenge – was not an easy process for him, just as it is not an easy one for us. The choice is always in our hands, but as we look at the face of Jesus and what He has done for us, that choice can soon be made. That process often doesn't come easily or quickly. But trusting in your forgiving God to walk you through the process will get you there in the end.

The thief, Satan, desires to steal, kill and destroy all that God has planned for good in your life. God's plan is for a life full of abundance and one that He has purposed for His Kingdom.

Joseph had no idea what God's plan for his life was on that day he found himself at the bottom of a dusty well. Betrayal after betrayal and pain, hurt and prison didn't deter his knowledge of who he served. His God's steadfast love was the refuge that lifted and molded him into the man that would be the best one for God's assignment. You stand in the same place: God's plan and assignment for your life is before you – your choice is to trust Him in the process.

Summary thought:

Joseph was able to declare, "God sent me to preserve life." That is an eternal mandate for each of us as we serve our Lord and Savior – Jesus Christ. Getting to our ultimate, completed assignment takes a lifetime of choices.

Those choices are to walk in a life full of continual love, forgiveness, compassion, kindness, humility and patience, along with many other attributes that He will knead into your heart, soul and mind. This kneading will always take place when you are quiet, separated, isolated – hidden in places where He can meet with you undistracted.

During these times He will transform you into the individual that He desires to use – leading you to His assignment, the very one that only you can perform.

Col. 3:12-14 Put on then, as God's chosen ones, holy and beloved, compassionate hearts, kindness, humility, meekness, and patience, bearing with one another and, if one has a complaint against another, forgiving each other; as the Lord has forgiven you, so you also must forgive. And above all these put-on love, which binds everything together in perfect harmony.

John 10:10 The thief comes only to steal and kill and destroy. I came that they may have life and have it abundantly.

Isa. 25:1 O Lord, you are my God I will exalt you; I will praise your name for you have done wonderful things, plans formed of old, faithful and sure.

Personal Insights:
_____
_____
_____
_____
_____
_____

H: How Does this Apply to Me?
_____
_____
_____
_____

O: Observations:
_____
_____
_____
_____

P: Personal Prayer:
_____
_____
_____
_____

E: Expression Through My Life (Action Step):
_____
_____
_____
_____

Chapter 5

Hidden to Spread the Gospel

Col. 1:27 To them God chose to make known how great among the Gentiles are the riches of the glory of this mystery, which is Christ in you, the hope of glory.

Hidden to Spread the Gospel

Stories from the Life of Paul

We live our lives, from young adulthood to our last breath as if we're running just ahead of dark clouds that are threatening to dump storms over us at any moment. Those storms come to us all, but the key to freedom is *how* we walk under the deluge.

Saul's life was changed in one blinding moment when he met Jesus on a dusty road. With a new name and a new purpose, his focus became one not of fear, but of freedom. He set the world on fire for the Gospel of Christ – never ceasing to declare the grace that had been freely given to him. Blinded but seeing, shipwrecked but faithful, imprisoned but content; he continued to grow through each storm, bringing freedom as he spread the Gospel.

Unshakeable faith, just like Paul's, allows a freedom for you to abide in the eye of the storm and still walk into every assignment God has called you to. Waiting out the squalls that surround you will strengthen your faith, and you may find great fruitfulness in the detours you didn't want and didn't expect to be part of your journey.

Blinded to See

The young man's anger grew as he stood in a group of respected leaders, transfixed by the audacity that came from this "disciple's" mouth. Stephen, a so-called disciple of Jesus, agitated Saul's thoughts as an internal demand for judgement rose within him, "This man and all those that believe these lies must be eradicated."

As stones, were picked up, one after another, his rage boiled up. He cheered as the disciple was stoned and took his last breath. His resolve to eliminate this new cult was solidified in his heart and mind as he determined, "This is my duty to God." With great zeal, Saul pursed the persecution of these people of "The Way," dragging men and women from their homes and imprisoning them with the hope of permanent elimination.

The day soon arrived when Saul's unrelenting passion for the blood of Christians could not be satisfied. He requested authorization to pursue the destruction of the cult beyond Jerusalem. With the approval of the leaders, he embarked on a journey to bring an end to these heretics – and he expected he would be extremely productive.

Saul began the trek with a group of strong, zealous men who were full of expectation and ready for retaliation. Instead of sucking out the murderous flame that now resided within him, the day's scorching heat seemed to ignite a personal wildfire that threatened to consume everything around him.

The target of his vengeance was within his sights as the city of Damascus appeared; that sight would soon be one of his last for a while.

In a sudden burst, a great flash of light erupted all around him – shaking him to his core. Falling to the ground, his mind swirled as he heard a booming voice, "Saul, Saul, why are you persecuting me?"

And Saul said, "Who are you, Lord?" And He said, "I am Jesus, whom you are persecuting. But rise and stand upon your feet, for I have appeared to you for this purpose, to appoint you as a servant and witness to the things in which you have seen me and to those in which I will appear to you, delivering you from your people and from the Gentiles – to whom I am sending you to open their eyes, so that they may turn from darkness to light and from the power of Satan to God, that they may receive forgiveness of sins, and a place among those who are sanctified by faith in me" (Acts 26: 16-18).

His men stood stunned, as they heard the voice but saw no one. They continued to tremble as Saul returned to his feet, covered in dust and completely blind. They whispered among themselves, "Who was that? What does this mean? Are we going to be blinded also?" No answer could be ascertained.

Saul was gripped with fear and could see nothing. His men apprehensively moved toward the city, leading him by the hand as if he were a child. This was not part of the plan! Finding a place to put away their previously-valiant leader, Saul's men left him alone; returning home disconcerted with their endeavor.

Blind, alone and residing in an unfamiliar city, and being cared for by unfamiliar people, he neither ate nor drank as he helplessly surrendered to God and listened intently for His voice. The thoughts, guilt and shame stirred in his heart as the reality of who Jesus was slipped in and transformation began its work. For three days he prayed and waited for whatever was to become of him.

While Saul blindly waited, God prepared another man to speak forgiveness and healing into his life. God directed Ananias to meet and declare freedom to this man who was a terror to his community.

He confirmed His request to Ananias, "Go, for he is a chosen instrument of mine to carry my name before the Gentiles and kings and the children of Israel. For I will show him how much he must suffer for the sake of my name" (Acts 9:15-16).

Ananias was faithful to God's direction and God moved mightily through him; allowing both forgiveness and healing to transform Saul as he was released from his blindness and scales fell from his eyes.

For several days he was strengthened and encouraged by the provision of the disciples of Damascus. They opened their hearts and lives to this man who, only days before, had come to kill them. A transformation in his life lit the passion that was housed within him and pointed it in a new direction. This direction would not only drive the gospel of Christ forward, but would also cause Saul to find himself headed into a life filled with turbulent storms.

(Enjoy reading the whole story in Acts 9:1-22)

Saul was a strongly religious, God-fearing man who, with great passion and zeal, pursued all that he knew was true. He was absolutely right in his eyes, and he was even right in the eyes of all those that he respected and spent time with. Yet, he was absolutely wrong!

We see what we think we see – but deception may be blinding our eyes. Not just in our spiritual life, but in every arena. There is a truth that is only found in Christ's truth: the truth that will set you free and allow the scales to fall from your eyes.

Just like Saul, we can already know God, but still be walking in deception. If you find yourself thinking that you have the *only right* answer (and everyone else is wrong), and *"Why can't they see what I see?"* continues to ring out in your mind: be aware that you may have some scales that Jesus wants to remove, too.

It is very easy to be swayed in our understanding of life. Every aspect of life – natural and spiritual – drives us to set up our own expectations. We have a predetermined idea of what we consider to be right and wrong in our work ethic, our money management and success, our child rearing, and our political affiliation and even in the details of our spiritual walk with Jesus.

Saul was right in *his* eyes, but he was wrong. His dramatic encounter with Jesus opened his eyes to the truth, but it required a time set aside – a time of hiding – where he laid down all his "right ideology" and looked into the eyes of Jesus. In that place (a surrendered, humble place) all deception fell off and freedom and joy erupted in his life, launching him into a new assignment that had been prepared for him.

When we surrender our fleshly thoughts, ideas and our *"we know it"* attitudes at the foot of the Cross, a realignment of our expectations begins. His promises and priorities become ours, and the transformation begun by the Spirit dissolves the scales from our eyes and our heart begins to soften.

Spending time at the feet of Jesus on a consistent basis changes everything: we find a new safe place – a place of abiding! With a softened, moldable heart, His revelations become our new truth and His priorities become ours. As you begin a new life in this place of abiding – waiting in His presence, humbly giving up your own thoughts and understanding – you become full of life, freedom and joy. Your life brings hope to others and the Gospel flows from you. It is all about a heart issue – as you lay down your opinions, His truth will set you free.

Summary thought:

Allowing the scales to be removed from your eyes and heart, seeing any aspect of life with newly-unveiled eyes and abiding continually in the presence of Jesus will bring a transformational paradigm shift – one that is only accomplished through the revelations that come from the hand of the Holy Spirit. Freedom comes when we see His way, not ours.

John 15:4 Abide in me, and I in you. As the branch cannot bear fruit by itself, unless it abides in the vine, neither can you, unless you abide in me.

John 8:31-32 So Jesus said to the Jews who had believed him, "If you abide in my word, you are truly my disciples, and you will know the truth and the truth will set you free."

Rom. 8:5 Those who are motivated by the flesh only pursue what benefits themselves. But those who live by the impulses of the Holy Spirit are motivated to pursue spiritual realities. (TPT)

Personal Insights:
___

H: How Does this Apply to Me?
___

O: Observations:
___

P: Personal Prayer:
___

E: Expression Through My Life (Action Step):
___

God's Planned Detour

With a new name and an ignited passion, Paul became the voice of the gospel to the Gentiles throughout the world. He never faltered in his declaration of the truth of the sonship of Jesus Christ and the freedom from sin that was purchased for all of mankind.

Twenty-three years of faithful travel and ministry had produced a prolifically strong church of believers. His life was filled with purpose as he preached freedom from sin that was found in the acceptance of a free, blood bought gift, given at the Cross, as Jesus exchanged His life for their life. Every corner of the continent soon was bathed in this joyous gift of salvation. But with growth came intimidation, as the same persecution Jesus experienced began to follow hard on his heels: imprisonment, beatings, taunting and false accusations seemed to await his arrival in every city.

On one day, just as the sun began to wane in Jerusalem, the religious debate over his teachings came to a clash. It grew violent and he was thrown into the barracks to await the morning's presentation of charges before the governor.

Tossing through the night, a major question stirred within his heart, "Is my mission for the Gospel complete?"

As the night hours grew quiet, a visitor arrived. Jesus appeared before him and said, "Take courage, for as you have testified to the facts about me in Jerusalem, so you must testify also in Rome" (Acts 23:11). His question was settled, and a new journey was to begin as he made his plea – as a Roman citizen – to stand in Rome to be judged.

The journey to carry Paul toward Rome by ship would be arduous at any time of year, but the ship's captain had determined to set sail at the end of the season, in hopes of beating the winter blast. The seas began to churn unrelentingly, making for "slow going." As ports and ships were changed, the weather continued to bear down on them.

About to leave yet another port, they readied the ship to move forward in search of a suitable harbor to anchor for the winter. Just before they launched out, Paul spoke up, "Sirs, I perceive that the voyage will be with injury and much loss, not only of the cargo and the ship, but also of our lives" (Acts 27: 10). But the centurion ignored him, and they set sail on the next juncture of the formidable journey.

The crisp morning held promise as the anchor was lifted. The sails unfurled with the gentle breeze, pulling them out into the sea. But without warning, the winds changed – becoming fierce, pushing and pulling them as water surged up and over the railings. Several days were spent fighting nature's fury but control was unattainable; they finally surrendered to the sea, allowing it to drive them forward.

The violent tossing continued without relief, water threatening to pull them under. By the third day, they began throwing cargo and tackle overboard, hoping to lighten the ship. Neither the sun nor stars where seen for days as they continued to be hammered by the elements; the wind's fierce power stirred the seas into a tempest as it drove sheets of drenching rain from the angry, dark clouds. As they continued their unrestrained battle with nature, hope of safely making land diminished. At last, all hope was gone and despair overcame them all.

God stirred Paul to restore hope to the exhausted and hungry crew. He stood up among them and said, "Men, you should have listened to me and not have set sail from Crete and incurred this injury and loss. Yet now I urge you to take heart for there will be no loss of life among you, but only of the ship. For this very night there stood before me an angel of the God to who I belong and whom I worship, and he said, 'Do not be afraid, Paul; you must stand before Caesar. And behold, God has granted you all those who sail with you.' So take heart, men, for I have faith in God that it will be exactly as I have been told. But we must run aground on some island" (Acts 27:21-26).

For several more days they continued to be driven forward by the storm, not knowing where they would end this turbulent journey. As the morning dawned, unfamiliar land came into sight – hope surged, yet getting there would require running the ship aground and trusting what Paul had declared, "No life would be lost."

The sound was deafening as the wood buckled, splintered and cracked; what was left of the cargo went flying and men were sent sprawling. The unavoidable "running aground" sounded better than the reality of "being shipwrecked." Either way, they hit the rocks and hit them hard. Swimming or floating on broken planks was their remaining mode of transportation as they arrived on an unfamiliar island with an unknown future looming before them. But they were all safe and alive, just as Paul had said. His God had been faithful, and His detour had landed Paul exactly where he was needed.

(Enjoy reading the whole story in Acts 21-27)

God's destinations in your life may require detours. When they occur, your endurance will be stretched and, at the same time, a preparation will take place for new growth. Detours always cause stress as we encounter the unknown and unfamiliar, fighting both internally and externally against them. Frustrations rise because we *think* we know our ultimate destination and *this* is not it!

Paul found himself right in the middle of a God detour and at the mercy of the decisions that others would make as he made his way toward what was his *planned destination*. For weeks, they battled the sea's fury as the ship was violently driven onto the rocks, bringing about a forced detour. What happened next allowed the gospel to be spread to a new people group that had been seeking God.

Hidden times of detour in your life require eyes open to God's plan. It may feel like a "shipwreck" to you, but if you allow the Holy Spirit to bring revelation and direction, you will begin to see that it can be used for His glory. Yield to His plans – not yours – as you anchor your hope to His faithful purpose in your life and for the Kingdom of God. He is your unshakeable hope; when life feels like a "shipwreck" has beached you, He has a greater plan.

Summary thought:

When the dark clouds and turbulence threaten to pull you under, reach up to the waiting hand of your Savior. Run into His arms – He is your anchor and hope. When hope is far from your own ability, trust that He does know, He does care and He does hear your call. He is only a whisper away. His plans for you may look as if they have been destroyed, but this is just a detour designed for His glory.

Heb. 6:18-20 So it is impossible for God to lie for we know that his promise and his vow will never change! And now we have run into his heart to hide ourselves in his faithfulness. This is where we find his strength and comfort, for he empowers us to seize what has already been established ahead of time—an unshakeable hope! We have this certain hope like a strong, unbreakable anchor holding
our souls to God himself. Our anchor of hope is fastened *to the mercy seat* which sits in the heavenly realm beyond the sacred threshold, and where Jesus, our forerunner, has gone in before us. He is now and forever our royal Priest like Melchizedek. (TPT)

Prov. 16:9 Within your heart you can make plans for your future, but the Lord chooses the steps you take to get there. (TPT)

Heb. 10:36 For you have need of endurance, so that when you have done the will of God you may receive what is promised.

Personal Insights:
_____
_____
_____
_____
_____
_____

H: How Does this Apply to Me?
_____
_____
_____
_____

O: Observations:
_____
_____
_____
_____

P: Personal Prayer:
_____
_____
_____
_____

E: Expression Through My Life (Action Step):
_____
_____
_____
_____

Contentment in a New Land

*A*long, difficult year was coming to an end as the port of Rome came into sight. Questions still unanswered, fleetingly circled his mind, "What lays ahead? How will God's plan play out before the Roman Gentiles?" His unknown fate hung in the balance, but his heart was at peace; his faith in God's plan and purpose for him was unshakable.

The last three months had quickly passed as he and the ship's crew wintered on the island of Malta. Preaching the gospel and healing many had produced a flourishing new church. As spring arrived, his heart was content on God's unexpected detour that had landed him here. However, it was time to continue his journey toward Rome. Paul's guard hitched a ride with another ship for the two of them, and they headed out toward their ultimate destination.

Paul continued to contemplate this unusual journey that had brought him to this new land. And now arriving in Rome, he stepped off the ship onto solid ground as God confirmed in his heart his mission. God had directed him to Rome, and every step was according to His plan – not Paul's. With anticipation of the spread of the gospel to the Roman Gentiles, he began a new opportunity in a new land.

Within a few days, he was able to gather the Jewish leaders and began to present the charges that had been falsely leveled against him, his defense and his declaration of Jesus. As he expounded the truths from the law of Moses, as well as the prophets, he continued to point them to the salvation offered by the blood of Christ – but most disagreed. As the discussion grew contentious, Paul declared in conclusion, "Therefore let it be known to you that this salvation of God has been sent to the Gentiles; they will listen" (Acts 28:28).

The leaders found no fault in Paul's teaching that was worthy of a sentence of death – but since he had requested the audience here in Rome, they felt they needed to keep him detained. As a political prisoner he was placed under house arrest, and he stayed in that position for over two years.

Contentment grew within Paul as months and years passed in Rome. He relished in the freedom offered to him, as he was afforded the ability to boldly preach without hindrance. Within his comfortable apartment, he was able to minister to visitors on a regular basis, as well as consistently write to the churches, encouraging and strengthening their faith continually. Here, hidden away, a contented heart spread the Gospel of Christ to the Gentiles and left an eternal legacy that fills the pages of the Bible with truth, faith, hope and wisdom.

(Enjoy reading the whole story in Acts 28)

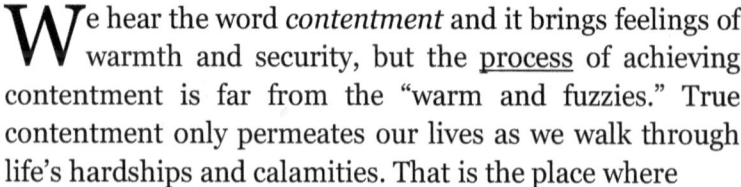

We hear the word *contentment* and it brings feelings of warmth and security, but the process of achieving contentment is far from the "warm and fuzzies." True contentment only permeates our lives as we walk through life's hardships and calamities. That is the place where endurance forges a strength within us to fight forward at whatever cost might be required.

As we look at Paul, we see that God took his previous training and talent, and in a blinding flash of light, gave him the choice to surrender to a new name and identity – one that God had planned in Heaven before he was born. That encounter would forever change him and the world, as he boldly spread the Gospel – preaching, teaching and writing.

If you are in the middle of cataclysmic circumstances and feel as if you are at the end of your own endurance, release your control into God's. With faith, reach out to Jesus – He is waiting to meet you right where you are.

As you surrender to a Holy Spirit encounter, He will stir a new-found endurance within you – one that can't be mustered up on your own, but one that requires an ignited flame and personal "flash of light" that is only found as you lean into His presence. At the feet of Jesus, you will find the strength and endurance to move forward – and as you do, contentment will begin to blossom.

Contentment arrives when you see your life through His eyes. As the endurance process continues, you will find yourself with a new name (identity) and a new purpose (God assignment). Your expectations will begin to realign with His and freedom will be released. You will become who He created you to be as you lay down your Saul and pick up your Paul. Then you will walk forward with unshakable faith, boldly proclaiming the freedom given to you through Jesus and living your life filled with contentment.

Summary thought:

The process of pressure and hardship, in a life surrendered to Christ, brings a determined endurance. That endurance allows for transformation from what was, into what is – an eternal purpose in life, and ultimately, a life filled with contentment. A life that spreads life and peace to those around it.

2 Cor. 12:10 For the sake of Christ, then, I am content with weaknesses, insults, hardships, persecutions, and calamities. For when I am weak, then I am strong.

2 Tim. 4:2 Proclaim the Word of God *and stand upon it no matter what*! Rise to the occasion and preach when it is convenient and when it is not. Preach in the full expression of the Holy Spirit—with wisdom and patience as you instruct and teach the people. (TPT)

1 Cor. 15:58 So now, beloved ones, stand firm and secure. Live your lives with an unshakable confidence. We know that we prosper and excel in every season by serving the Lord, because we are assured that our union with the Lord makes our labor productive with fruit that endures. (TPT)

Personal Insights:
_____
_____
_____
_____
_____
_____
_____

H: How Does this Apply to Me?
_____
_____
_____
_____

O: Observations:
_____
_____
_____
_____

P: Personal Prayer:
_____
_____
_____
_____

E: Expression Through My Life (Action Step):
_____
_____
_____
_____

Chapter 6

Hidden to Become King

John 16:33 I have said these things to you, that in me you may have peace. In the world you will have tribulation. But take heart; I have overcome the

Hidden to Become King

Stories from the Life of David

It is every parent's desire to infuse integrity in their children and to see that character trait mature in them as they grow. The very definition of "integrity" speaks of honesty, soundness of moral character and an unwavering adherence to both moral and ethical principles. Yet today, the very word "integrity" has begun to shift toward a negative interpretation. Sighs, smirks and eye rolls commonly occur when the phrase *a man of integrity* is spoken. Why? Because our society has begun to see a loss of honesty, truth and virtue that is so great that instead of seeking after this trait, we belittle its true intent. Integrity has become a negative *tagline.*

What does this have to do with the story of David? A lot! As a young boy, David was known to God as *a man after his own heart.* From a worshiping shepherd boy to a stone-slinging giant-killer, from a warrior to a commander, from a cave dweller to the throne: David was a man of integrity. Yes, he did make mistakes and he did sin – but with humility, his heart always turned back to God. David was a true example of what the word "integrity" means. And God loved David, forgiving his human indiscretions because He knew him (even though lust, adultery and murder came to the top of David's *sin* list). His very core held a deep integrity of character and a yielded spirit.

Let's look at this trait a little closer as we read a few stories about David's life. Perhaps your understanding of integrity can be shifted back to its original intent.

A Sheepfold's Refuge

As midnight's darkness engulfed the young boy, a slight breeze blew over the rocks stirring a puff of dust and with it came the scent of danger that only the sleeping sheep detected. Their movement and bleating alerted David, and with his staff in hand he circled the sheepfold making himself as loud and big as possible for a twelve-year-old boy. The sheep relaxed and huddled back together, ready to sleep a little more before sunrise. "This time must have been a false alarm," He thought.

David settled back to rest, but thoughts circled in his mind. He remembered close calls and other losses, when much more than a walk around the sheepfold had been required. More than once he had fought off lions and bears, ripping broken and bleeding sheep from their clutches and their dead jaws. His strength and alertness had grown as he experienced each deadly encounter.

It was at an early age that he learned his peace came from worshiping his God. Tonight, as his thoughts spun into concerns, out came his harp and his heart turned toward the heavens in music – soothing both his heart and his sheep. Shortly, the filtering light of sunrise grew into a glorious day as God's peace drove away fear and loneliness that had lurked beside him throughout the dark night.

Today as David was busy caring for the sheep, his father and brothers had been summoned to join the prophet in order to participate in a sacrifice. Since David was the youngest, it was not unusual for him to be left out of these commitments. The truth was that he was happy to be left to peacefully wander the hills with his sheep. In this safe, hidden-away place, David found a refuge of tranquility. But today would be different.

He saw his father's servant swiftly approaching him as he motioned for him to come and hurry home; the servant assured David that he would take his place with the sheep, for his father was calling him to join the family immediately. As he instantly obeyed, his strong legs jumped into action, leaving his mind the freedom to wonder about this sudden turn in his day, "What could the prophet want with me?"

God's prophet, Samuel, had been sent to anoint one of Jesse's sons as Israel's next king, and he faithfully listened for God's voice as each son was presented. All of them appeared to be strong and able to lead in this great commission, yet God said, "Do not look on the appearance or on the height of stature. For I see not as man sees. Man looks on the outward appearance, but the Lord looks on the heart."

David arrived home breathless and sweaty, finding the entire household standing and waiting for his arrival. As he was presented before the prophet, the Lord spoke to Samuel, "Arise, anoint him, for this is he" (1 Sam. 16:12b).

Samuel came forward and poured anointing oil over David's head as his father and older brothers watched in astonishment. The prophet declared David to be king over Israel, and the Spirit of the Lord rushed upon him, and continued to hover over him from that day forward.

David continued caring for the sheep, while a warrior's strength and abilities grew evermore obvious and his love and worship for his God flourished in the quiet, lonely hills.

However, he still wondered about that day the prophet had arrived and the events that had transpired, but for now his focus was on this assignment before him: to care and protect his father's sheep. What was to come? That was in God's hands.

(Enjoy reading the whole story 1 Sam. 16:1-13)

Chaos seems to wait for us at every turn, we open our eyes every morning unsure of the next life-impacting change that will transpire before we sleep tonight. Yet sleep still alludes us, as worries and concerns replay in our minds. Does that sound familiar?

At twelve years old, David encountered the same. He was given an assignment that carried with it long, lonely nights, physical labor and lurking eminent danger. He learned to be strong when he felt weak, to push through hard things and dig deep within himself and to fight forward when he wanted to run. This assignment taught him God's faithfulness and prepared him, from a very early age, to trust that he was not really alone, not on his own and not forgotten. He came to know his God intimately through those lonely nights and he felt His presence alongside him as he cared and tended to his little flock, and even while burying those he lost. And when fear crept in, he chose to fix his eyes on his faithful God: singing, worshiping and making music.

David probably brought an instrument to his sheepfold to give him something to occupy his time in those long nights, but soon it became an imperative and lifelong tool that brought him and others solace and entrance into the very presence of God. Our place of singing, music and worship can do the same. Try it out: when fears, loneliness and struggles surround you, lift your voice to Heaven and watch as God dissolves your cares.

David's nights were much like ours, but he found an answer – a place of refuge and a place that brought peace – and it was found in worship. This place of worship is where we can find the same refuge; where peace will reign in the midst of the chaos and where we can meet and build a strong personal relationship with Jesus Christ: the same faithful God that David knew. Remembering as in Heb. 13:8, *Jesus Christ is the same yesterday and today and forever*

The plans that God had for David required learning this foundational truth: *you shall love the Lord your God with all your heart and with all your soul and with all your mind and with all your strength* (Mark 12:30). He learned this while he was all alone out in the sheepfold – all alone singing and worshiping to his God. God met David there and He saw his heart. God knew that he would be a man who would serve Him and Him only. David's identity and assignment were pre-determinedly set in Heaven, and he chose to yield to God's plans and purposes.

How is God using these times of chaos, fear, loneliness and loss in your life to shape who you are becoming? What assignment is waiting for you to step into? Remember, waiting and listening are the keys. Don't circumvent the <u>waiting process</u>! Attaining this assignment requires hanging out in the sheepfold – the place where trusting in His plan and timing, leaning into His presence and learning to worship at His feet will bring about His plan and timing. David tenaciously fought, courageously protected and lived a life faithful to the assignment God placed before him – let's do the same.

<u>Summary thought:</u>

Setting your focus on trusting in God's faithfulness, while you love Him with all your heart, mind, soul and strength, will produce a yielded life. You can set aside the world's spinning chaos, finding refuge under His wings when you worship – truly laying down your cares at His feet. From that place, you will move into the assignment He has set before you, walking in today – not rushing toward tomorrow – knowing what is to come is in God's hands.

<u>Isa. 41:10</u> Do not yield to fear, for I am always near. Never turn your gaze from me, for I am your *faithful* God. I will infuse you with my strength and help you in every situation. I will hold you firmly with my victorious right hand.' (TPT)

<u>Ps. 71:22</u> My loving God, the harp in my heart will praise you. Your faithful heart toward us will be the theme of my song. Melodies and music will rise to you, the Holy One of Israel. (TPT)

Luke 16:10 The one who manages the little he has been given with faithfulness and integrity will be promoted and trusted with greater responsibilities. But those who cheat with the little they have been given will not be considered trustworthy to receive more. (TPT)

Personal Insights:
_____
_____
_____
_____
_____
_____

H: How Does this Apply to Me?
_____
_____
_____
_____

O: Observations:
_____
_____
_____
_____

P: Personal Prayer:
_____
_____
_____
_____

E: Expression Through My Life (Action Step):
_____
_____
_____
_____

Overcoming a Giant

Several years had passed as David continued to tend sheep, all the while growing into a strong, young man and becoming known throughout the kingdom for his musical ability. When King Saul began to struggle with mental torment and desired to gain relief, his servant announced, "Behold, I have seen a son of Jesse the Bethlehemite, who is skilled in playing, a man of valor, a man of war, prudent in speech, and a man of good presence, and the Lord is with him" (1 Sam. 16:18). David's name was now at the top of Saul's list.

Saul soon sent for David to enter his service and requested his harp playing, hoping to soothe the torment that often settled over him. The presence of the Lord was evident over the life of David, and every aspect of his integrity shined out before him.

His arrival to the court brought a much needed "presence of the Lord" into the throne room, and quickly Saul grew to count on David. Saul's trust and love for this young musician increased, placing him into a close and personal position – the king's armor-bearer.

Still honoring his father, he would travel home to care for the sheep and care for his other needs. Unbeknownst to him, today's errand would catapult him into the obvious forefront of the kingdom.

Saul, along with his battle warriors, had been fighting the Philistines for forty days in the valley of Elah. As days with no word dragged on, David's father became concerned for the welfare of his three eldest sons who had joined the army. Equipping him with grain, bread and cheese, he requested that David run these supplies to the front lines and check on them.

The day grew hot as David traveled toward the battle arena, but this was an exciting change of pace from this sixteen-year-old's normal activities, and with every mile an unexplainable anticipation began to grow within him. As he approached the encampment, he heard the clanking of metal as armor, shields and boots moved toward the battle lines and the eruption of shouts of war filled the air. He dropped off the supplies he had been entrusted with at the rear, then moved with agility toward the front lines, weaving through the clamoring mass of preparation. Making swift headway, he found his brothers and excitedly inquired about the battle's progress.

Silence fell over the field, as a massive, nine-foot-tall Philistine warrior stepped toward Israel's battle line. This was not the first time Saul's men had encountered Goliath, for he had already taunted them. But it was the first time that David had heard this giant give his degrading battle challenge. He stood and shouted to the ranks of Israel, "Why have you come out to draw up for battle? Am I not a Philistine, and are you not servants of Saul? Choose a man for yourselves, and let him come down to me. If he is able to fight with me and kill me, then we will be your servants. But if I prevail against him and kill him, then you shall be our servants and serve us." And the Philistine said, "I defy the ranks of Israel this day. Give me a man, that we may fight together" (1 Sam. 17:8-10). Upon hearing this declaration, Israel's warriors again became fearful and fled the presence of Goliath as he continued to taunt them.

Indignation rose within David and he spoke with confidence to the men around him. His brothers and many other warriors became angry with David, "You are just a child! Who are you to question our battle ability?"

Soon the words and questions that David had spoken reached the ears of Saul, and he found himself before the king. Without hesitation, David asserted his willingness to fight the giant, but Saul also discouraged him because of his youth and inexperience. Yet, without a tested armor, David walked out onto the battlefield with only five smooth stones and a slingshot.

Goliath scoffed at the possibility that Israel would send an unarmed boy out to meet him, and he cursed David and his God. With great faith and courage, David stepped up and responded, "You come to me with a sword and with a spear and with a javelin, but I come to you in the name of the Lord of hosts, the God of the armies of Israel, whom you have defied. This day the Lord will deliver you into my hand, and I will strike you down and cut off your head. And I will give the dead bodies of the host of the Philistines this day to the birds of the air and to the wild beasts of the earth, that all the earth may know that there is a God in Israel, and that all this assembly may know that the Lord saves not with sword and spear. For the battle is the Lord's, and he will give you into our hand" (1 Sam. 17:45-47).

David didn't have time to think about what would transpire in the next few minutes – he just trusted that His God was with him and this giant was no different from the lions or the bears that threatened to decimate his flock. He ran toward the giant, pulled a single smooth stone from his pouch and shot it from his slingshot – landing it perfectly into the giant's skull and sending him facedown into the dirt. With a swift movement, he lifted the heavy sword from Goliath's still body and swung it with great force, removing the Philistines head from his shoulders.

This day changed a boy into a warrior – pulling him from obscurity, and thrusting him into a new trajectory toward the throne.

(Enjoy reading the whole story in 1 Sam. 16:14-23, 17:1-58)

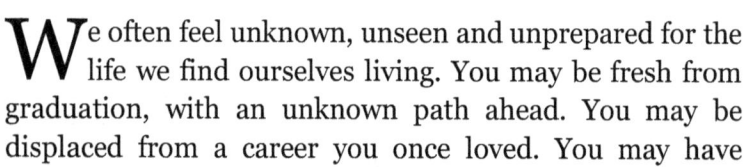

We often feel unknown, unseen and unprepared for the life we find ourselves living. You may be fresh from graduation, with an unknown path ahead. You may be displaced from a career you once loved. You may have retired and feel useless with no purpose left. Or you may find yourself anywhere in between. But today, realize that God does see you and is preparing you for a purpose that still lies ahead – one that He knows all about.

David used what he was given, a harp and a heart to worship, and suddenly found himself in the king's court. Hidden in plain site, at the right hand of the king, God began a job-shadowing program for David. Wisdom and understanding grew within this shepherd boy as faith and courage took root. And as an unexpected opportunity arose, all that had been hidden exploded forth as a smooth stone met its mark – taking down a giant.

What giant stands looming over you today? Find hope, courage and faith to step out at just the right time, and stand up and take down that giant in the name of Jesus Christ. We are overcomers!

The battle must still be fought and a few scars may be acquired, but God has a plan and purpose for your life. He knows that plan; He sees you and He has been preparing you. Don't falter, hide or think you are too young or too old – instead, pick up what He has already given you and fight forward. As written in John 10:10, God's intention is to give you a life full of abundance (a life with special advantage) a life willing and able to overcome all that would love to kill, rob or steal from you.

Yes, use that talent or gift – that part of you that you think is *just you*. It is you, but He has put it in your life to be used. You are shaped, molded and prepared from your mother's womb for God's great intentions – intentions that He has given to you for a life overflowing for His glory.

Even those difficult, life-changing events that you think will destroy you? Yes, He can redeem those and turn them into opportunities that will bring freedom, encouragement and eternal life through you and into those around you, all for God's glory.

Summary thought:

Winning the battle and becoming a victorious child of the King of kings is determined by your choices, attitudes and yielded heart as you walk through your life. You can run away, hide, and allow anger and bitterness to take root OR you can run headlong into the battle, knowing that it belongs to the Lord. If you find yourself in front of the giant – choose faith and determine to be an overcomer today.

Col. 2:6-7 In the same way you received Jesus our Lord and Messiah by faith, continue your journey of faith, progressing further into your union with him! Your spiritual roots go deeply into his life as you are continually infused with strength, encouraged in every way. For you are established in the faith you have absorbed and enriched by your devotion to him! (TPT)

Prov. 2:1-5 My son, if you receive my words and treasure up my commandments with you, making your ear attentive to wisdom and inclining your heart to understanding; yes, if you call out for insight and raise your voice for understanding, if you seek it like silver and search for it as for hidden treasures, then you will understand the fear of the Lord and find the knowledge of God.

Ps. 20:7 Some find their strength in their weapons and wisdom, but my miracle deliverance can never be won by men. Our boast is in the Lord our God, who makes us strong and gives us victory! (TPT)

Personal Insights:
_____
_____
_____
_____
_____
_____

H: How Does this Apply to Me?
_____
_____
_____
_____

O: Observations:
_____
_____
_____
_____

P: Personal Prayer:
_____
_____
_____
_____

E: Expression Through My Life (Action Step):
_____
_____
_____
_____

The King's Warrior

Finding himself ejected from the king's presence was unsettling for David. For many years he had helped soothe Saul's mental struggles and had given him advice, as well as became best friends with his son, Jonathan. He faithfully stood beside him through the trials and triumphs and even had his eye on Saul's daughter, with hopes of making her his bride. But jealousy raged within Saul, and David's strong bond and friendship with his son and the people's celebration over the slaying of Goliath continued to fuel it. Without warning, David found himself removed from the courts.

He was now set as a commander over a thousand warriors that went out and came in on behalf of the king, but was not in contact with him. David accepted his new assignment with the strength and tenacity that his integrity and faith in God had prepared him for from his youth. God's presence continued to surround him as he directed battle after battle with wisdom and success.

Saul's removal of David's presence from the court relieved one internal battle, but seeing his success and obvious favor of God in the battlefield stirred up another. Fear of David's success began to raise its head as the tormentor seethed within Saul's mind.

Battles continued to rage around Israel that required strong wisdom and leadership, and each one brought success as David proved himself a mighty man of valor. With each victory, he received admiration and respect from both his men and the people of the land.

Though David stayed hidden away from the presence of Saul, his reputation made itself known in the court – Godly success has a way of doing that. The stories of David's exploits drove Saul into a frenzy, pushing him to contrive a murderous plot to kill him, using the temptation of his own daughter as a bribe.

David had fallen in love with Saul's daughter, Michal, and was overjoyed when the king's servant brought him an offer to become the king's son-in-law. His joy was short-lived as he realized he had no bride-price, for he was a poor man. However, Saul's devious thoughts bloomed into action as he proclaimed, "The king desires no bride-price except one hundred foreskins of the Philistines, that he may be avenged of the king's enemies." Saul was hoping that David would fall at the hands of one of those one hundred Philistines and he would be rid of him.

The next morning, David rose early. He and his men began what would become a bloody battle, and he ended it with taking the lives of 200 Philistines – twice what had been required. Those bloody foreskins became the price of David's bride. Saul honored this agreement; he gave Michal to David as his wife, and David became Saul's son-in-law. What Saul had hoped to be the end of David, instead became one more valiant triumph to be cheered through the streets and solidified David as his enemy that now continually stood before him.

(Enjoy reading the whole story in 1 Sam. 18)

As our society struggles with making sense of devastating losses that haven't been experienced to the current extreme for decades, we cannot help but find ourselves with questions, frustrations and discouragement knocking at the door of our hearts and minds. If you find yourself there, you are not alone.

David found himself removed from the king's court after years of faithful service. He had done nothing wrong to warrant the change in his situation. He was hidden away from all of what had been his normal life and placed into an isolated position. I'm sure he struggled with questions, frustrations and discouragement. Yet, he shook it off and walked into his new assignment – his new normal – expecting God to continue in faithfulness on his behalf.

During times of struggles – where the pressure is on – we are prepared and stretched. Our roots are required to push deeper, for that is where new growth – stronger, more productive growth – is found.

David found courage rise up as he prepared to lead his men into battle after battle. He became known for his valor, courage and integrity. God was preparing him to step into a role – a role where only the pressure of battle could prepare him.

Don't despair if you feel as if you have lost your footing in the life you thought you had all planned out. Find hope in knowing that your God is faithful, that He does have a plan and that His plan requires some battles. These battles are the preparation that will ignite courage and strength within you. They will train a deep integrity and fortitude to rise up as you resiliently move forward. And these battles will draw others to you – they will see something and will desire to receive what you are carrying.

And what is that you are carrying? You are carrying the reality of who Jesus is, in and through your life – and that is the identity that will become a story of truth and eternal transformation as you walk in life as a warrior for the King.

Summary thought:

Wherever you go, whatever battle you face and whenever changes erupt around you: take courage, be strong, shake off discouragement and know that God is for you, not against you. You are a representative of the Kingdom of God – His beloved child – and He has a plan and purpose as He is preparing you to enter into it. Don't become battle-weary in the process; pick up your weapons (Worship, God's Word and Warfare prayer) and know that He is the victor in your life.

Josh. 1:9 Have I not commanded you? Be strong and courageous. Do not be frightened, and do not be dismayed, for the Lord your God is with you wherever you go."

Ps. 42:5 Then I will say to my soul, "Don't be discouraged; don't be disturbed, for I fully expect my Savior-God to break through for me. Then I'll have plenty of reasons to praise him all over again." Yes, living before his face is my saving grace! (TPT)

Ps. 18:34 You've trained me with the weapons of warfare-worship; now I'll descend into battle with power to chase and conquer my foes. (TPT)

Personal Insights:
_____
_____
_____
_____
_____
_____

H: How Does this Apply to Me?
_____
_____
_____
_____

O: Observations:
_____
_____
_____
_____

P: Personal Prayer:
_____
_____
_____
_____

E: Expression Through My Life (Action Step):
_____
_____
_____
_____

Compassionate Cave-dweller

*I*n an instant, the mood in the room changed from peaceful to murderous as rage erupted from Saul. A spear thundered past David's head – landing with deadly intent, deep into the wall. Saul was determined to kill him, and David ran for his life. When he arrived home, his wife had already heard of the king's outburst and declaration to kill him. She encouraged David that he must leave to save his life, "If you do not escape with your life tonight, tomorrow you will be killed." The soldiers were headed his way, so they quickly prepared a deception to buy some time. Michal let David down through the window and he fled off into the night.

Running and hiding became the norm for David for several years, as he continued to elude Saul's hunt. The dark, damp life of a cave dweller was not what he had imagined his path to becoming Israel's king would include, yet here he found himself. News of his plight reached his family and they journeyed to join him. And as word continued to spread, soon everyone who was in distress, in debt or heartsick over the depravity of their nation all gathered with David.

As commander over his four hundred faithful men, the hunted, nomadic life continued for this newly-formed band. Battle after battle raged as separation, deprivation and hunger began to numb him. But he knew that His God was faithful and true, and he would worship even in the midst of the darkest nights.

News of David's whereabouts reached Saul, and with three thousand men he pursued him and the men who followed him – determined to kill them all. The trek was through the hills and rocky country, requiring slow and difficult, steep hiking. Traversing and searching for this little band of the "dredges of society" caused Saul's men to grow weary and set aside their vigilante alertness. When the day became stifling, Saul spied a cave that would meet his physical needs. He climbed over the rocks and entered alone, completely off guard and unaware that David and his men sat in the innermost parts of that very cave.

Whispering to David, his men encouraged him, "Here is the day of which the Lord said to you, 'Behold, I will give your enemy into your hand, and you shall do to him as it shall seem good to you'" (1 Sam. 24:4). David snuck up behind Saul as he sat vulnerable and exposed and cut off a corner of his robe.

But as he returned to his men, the Spirit of the Lord filled him with deep regret and David said, "The Lord forbid that I should do this thing to my lord, the Lord's anointed, to put out my hand against him, seeing he is the Lord's anointed" (1 Sam. 24:6). David persuaded his men not to attack Saul, but to trust in God's timing in the removal of Saul from the throne. David did not want Saul's blood on his hands, nor did he want to run ahead of God's predetermined plan.

As Saul left the cave, returning to his men and his hunt for David, a voice came from the very cave he had just left, "My Lord the king!" Instantly on guard, Saul turned ready for battle, but found David bowed with his face to the earth. David, holding up the piece of cloth cut from Saul's robe, said, "See, my father, see the corner of your robe in my hand. For by the fact that I cut off the corner of your robe and did not kill you, you may know and see that there is no wrong or treason in my hands. I have not sinned against you, though you hunt my life to take it" (1 Sam. 24:11).

Saul wept and said, "You have declared this day how you have dealt well with me, in that you did not kill me when the Lord put me into your hands. And now, behold, I know that you shall surely be king, and that the kingdom of Israel shall be established in your hand" (1 Sam. 24:18,20).

Yet Saul was easily swayed and manipulated toward the bitterness, anger and jealousy that reigned within his spirit, and soon he pursued David again. And again, God gave David an opportunity to take Saul's life – this time as Saul slept. But David once again refused to pour out revenge; taking only his spear, he declared that Saul would not fall by his hand.

Compassion and forgiveness continued to win over the need for revenge in David's life as he and his men lived battle-to-battle, waiting for God's timing. And just as David had declared, Saul died at the hands of Israel's enemy in the middle of battle, making room for David's ascent from cave to throne.

(Enjoy reading the whole story in 1 Sam. 19-24)

The voices that surge around us today seethe with anger, hate and bitterness, as revenge and justice are continually shouted from the airwaves and protesters in every city. It is easy to be influenced by these cries. It is easy to join those voices with our own adamant opinions. It is not easy to turn this tide – to speak life, kindness and grace. Yet, that is what we are called to do.

David was forced to hide in damp, dark caves, hungry and isolated. Yet when opportunity arose, he chose – yes, he *chose* – to show compassion, not revenge. Justice was not found; instead, forgiveness rose as he humbly bowed to the dirt before the king. Calling the king "my father" dissipated a hateful spirit from a vengeful king.

As the church, we are the Bride of Christ. The Church that Jesus Christ called to walk in grace, love, compassion and forgiveness. We have to choose to put aside the judgement that society rants out at us. We must choose to not speak or post online the same divisive words, but instead speak or post only kindness and grace.

David had every right to declare justice be served and to take the life of this man who was bent on killing him. Yet he chose to be a man after God's own heart, a man with integrity, a man of compassion and a man that God would place on the throne – not by his hand or timing, but by God's alone.

We are to be different from the world. Our identity has been redeemed from the womb, just as David's was. How we express that identity is a choice that can change the environment we live in. We can shout in judgement for revenge and justice: Or we can show the world a different Spirit! A Spirit of compassion, forgiveness, grace, mercy and love – like our Savior's.

Summary thought:

Let's come out of the damp, dark cave where we have joined with the world, and become the light of Christ and bring His forgiveness. Make a choice to move from the cave to the foot of the cross, where humility meets forgiveness and freedom. There we will find the ability to walk forward as He has called us, bringing light to a dark world.

Ps. 57:1 Be merciful to me, O God, be merciful to me, for in you my soul takes refuge; in the shadow of your wings I will take refuge, till the storms of destruction pass by.

Eph. 4:31-32 Lay aside bitter words, temper tantrums, revenge, profanity, and insults. But instead be kind and affectionate toward one another. Has God graciously forgiven you? Then graciously forgive one another in the depths of Christ's love. (TPT)

Jer. 1:5 Before I formed you in the womb I knew you, and before you were born I consecrated you; I appointed you a prophet to the nations."

Personal Insights:

_____
_____
_____
_____
_____
_____

H: How Does this Apply to Me?

_____
_____
_____
_____

O: Observations:

_____
_____
_____
_____

P: Personal Prayer:

_____
_____
_____
_____

E: Expression Through My Life (Action Step):

_____
_____
_____
_____

Chapter 7

Hidden for God's Perfect Time

J. K. Sanchez

Eccles. 3:1 For everything there is a season, and a time for every matter under heaven:

Hidden for God's Perfect Time

Stories from the lives of Esther, Noah and Jonah

Early in life, we learn to hide things. We put them away to keep them safe and to use them at *just the right time*. Everything we hide away is a treasure we care for, a treasure that we expect will eventually *do great things for us*. Well, God is the perfect example of this process. He often hides us away, keeping us safe and preparing us – to be used at *just the right time*.

Preparation of each of His treasure's requires different processes and various lengths of time to be ready for its specific use. But the plan is to use each treasure in a special way – a special way that only *it* can accomplish. That is who you are: God's special treasure that He is preparing for the assignment that only *you* can accomplish.

God's perfect timing comes when we are made ready – when we are molded into the treasure that shines for His glory. Humility must be refined, and obedience and wisdom become honored attributes. Grace and mercy must be understood, as forgiveness becomes our cornerstone. Our listening ears must tune into His voice, and holiness will become a trusted covering. Our faith will erupt, thrusting us past belief and into a steadfast focus – a focus that will have us ready to pick up the designated tools and go to work when He gives us direction.

From delivering a nation to building an ark, and even from the bottom of the sea in the belly of a giant fish, we see God's hand creating treasures that He hides, making them ready for His perfect time – His perfect assignment.

"For Such a Time"

Young and vulnerable, she found herself in King Ahasuerus' court with all the chaos, rules and glamour that came along with it. Her uncle, Mordecai, had loved and cared for her after her parents died, and as she entered the palace he instructed her to keep her heritage a secret – no one knew that she was a Jew. Her stunning figure, hair and complexion caught the king's eye, and a yearlong preparation began as she was readied to come before him. When her year of preparation was complete, she was called to the king where she found favor in his heart.

The king loved Esther, and soon the young woman's beauty went before her as the crown was placed on her head. This young, orphaned Jewish woman had won the favor and heart of the king, becoming the queen.

Haman, an official of the king, also grew in the king's favor and became powerful as he was put in charge of much of the kingdom's daily operations. He gloried in the praise and adoration that surrounded him, soon demanding those in his presence to bow before him.

But there was a man, Mordecai, who refused – his worship and praise was to be given to only one, his God. This refusal angered Haman. Finding that Mordecai was a Jew and that the Jews would not worship or praise anyone but their God, Haman determined to destroy not only Mordecai, but all the Jews.

Filled with deception, Haman went before the king with a request. Then Haman said to King Ahasuerus, "There is a certain people scattered abroad and dispersed among the peoples in all provinces of your kingdom. Their laws are different from those of every other people, and they do not keep the king's laws, so that it is not to the king's profit to tolerate them. If it pleases the king, let it be decreed that they be destroyed, and I will pay 10,000 talents of silver into the hands of those who have charge of the king's business, that they may put it into the king's treasuries" (Est. 3:8-9).

The king agreed to Haman's request; a decree was made, and letters were sent throughout the kingdom calling for the destruction of all the Jews. Chaos and confusion surged as these orders and plans were made, and there was great mourning in the land. Prayers and fasting erupted from the condemned people, and Esther heard the pandemonium that began to rise through her windows and was distressed upon hearing its cause.

Mordecai sent word to Esther, requesting her help. He asked that she go to the king to beg for his favor and plead with him on behalf of her people. Fear leapt within Esther as she heard this request.

Worries and fears circled in her mind, "How could I go before the king and request such a thing?" The king doesn't even know that I, too, am a Jew. Doesn't Mordecai know that for me to go before the king unannounced is certain death? Even if I did, the king hasn't called for me for more than thirty days – he could choose to not extent his golden scepter and forbid me to talk." All of her opposition quickly came to an end when Mordecai's message arrived.

Mordecai told them to reply to Esther, "Do not think to yourself that in the king's palace, you will escape any more than all the other Jews. For if you keep silent at this time, relief and deliverance will rise for the Jews from another place, but you and your father's house will perish. And who knows whether you have not come to the kingdom for such a time as this?" (Est. 4:13-14).

Upon receiving Mordecai's message, all of Esther's opposition quickly came to an end, resolve settling within her spirit as faith took hold. She requested that the Jews of the kingdom join her in three days of fasting and prayer; at the end of that time she would go before the king with the request. Trusting in her God, she decided that if she perished in the process, she would have at least done all she could. They embarked on three days of prayer and fasting as Esther prepared her heart to step before the king. She trusted that she was in God's hands as she began her walk toward the throne room.

With great wisdom, Esther prepared an elaborate plan to honor the king. But she knew she first had to get through the doors and into the inner courts of the throne room – unannounced. With a deep breath and all the regality of a queen, she stepped in. To her relief, the king extended the golden scepter to her to come forward, his gaze expressing the love and favor he found in her.

She was accepted into his presence, but winning the salvation of her people would require wisdom and humility. The king made a move toward her and she accepted. For several days she asked only for more time *with him. Then when the time was right, she revealed Haman's plot and deception, her identity as a Jew and her request for the removal of the decree to execute her people. God's mighty hand had worked behind the scenes to prepare the king's heart by giving him a sleepless night and placing specific reading material into his hands that would determine his decision. In the end, all these things brought about honor for Mordecai, destruction for Haman and the salvation of the Jewish nation.*

(Enjoy reading the whole story in Esther 1-10)

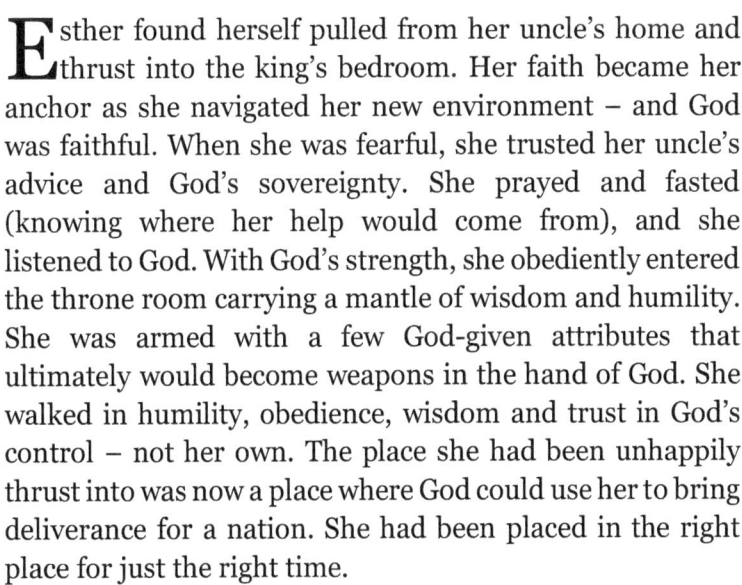

Esther found herself pulled from her uncle's home and thrust into the king's bedroom. Her faith became her anchor as she navigated her new environment – and God was faithful. When she was fearful, she trusted her uncle's advice and God's sovereignty. She prayed and fasted (knowing where her help would come from), and she listened to God. With God's strength, she obediently entered the throne room carrying a mantle of wisdom and humility. She was armed with a few God-given attributes that ultimately would become weapons in the hand of God. She walked in humility, obedience, wisdom and trust in God's control – not her own. The place she had been unhappily thrust into was now a place where God could use her to bring deliverance for a nation. She had been placed in the right place for just the right time.

We often move through life on *autopilot* – but what happens when we suddenly find everything interrupted, and the life we thought we had, or would have, are drastically altered? Have you found yourself asking, "Now what?" That question has been uttered by most of the world recently, as so much that was once "normal" has now changed. How we look at it and respond needs to be shaken up and adjusted, driving us to find a new perspective.

When we encounter life interruptions, we, like Esther, have choices to make. Yes – fears jump in and frustrations rise, and we want to bury our heads in the sand and pretend it is not happening. But your best answer is found in choosing to intentionally put the brakes on and spend time at the feet of Jesus.

Prayer was Esther's first *call to arms;* in this place of prayer, you, too, can give up your control and accept God's control over your situation. You will find that when you look up, He will provide the answer; He knows exactly where you are. But next, you must lay down your *expected* answers. Humility says, "It's your call God, even if the answer is, 'no.'"

If we humbly accept the place we find ourselves in, ask for His direction and obediently move as He instructs, we may suddenly find that He has hidden us in this place for a purpose that could not be fulfilled without this unexpected "life interruption."

Summary thought:

Just like Esther, we are being prepared to be the bride that He is returning for. But that preparation requires times of stretching, times of humbling, and times – extended times – at the feet of Jesus. These times are when our faith must rise up as we step out of our comfort zone and boldly walk into the places God has called us to – even those we really don't want to go into.

His purpose for your life is to use you for His glory, and that will require walking in humility and obedience, listening to His voice, speaking with His wisdom and boldly saying, "Yes, Lord." Your hidden "life-interruption" might be the place He has chosen to bring a glorious deliverance, or the place He has allowed to prepare you to shine forth His glory in His timing.

1 Pet. 5:6 Humble yourselves, therefore, under the mighty hand of God so that at the proper time he may exalt you,

Jer. 7:23 But this command I gave them: 'Obey my voice, and I will be your God, and you shall be my people. And walk in all the way that I command you, that it may be well with you.'

Rev. 19:7 Let us rejoice and exult and give him the glory, for the marriage of the Lamb has come, and his Bride has made herself ready;

Personal Insights:
_____
_____
_____
_____
_____
_____

H: How Does this Apply to Me?
_____
_____
_____
_____

O: Observations:
_____
_____
_____
_____

P: Personal Prayer:
_____
_____
_____
_____

E: Expression Through My Life (Action Step):
_____
_____
_____
_____

God's New Beginning

*C*haos, violence and debauchery of every kind grew throughout the world. It had ignited to a crescendo that God could no longer tolerate, and His heart grieved that He had made man on the earth.

But there was one man, Noah, who God found favor in. He spoke with Noah and had friendship with him. So, before God destroyed all that He had created, He warned Noah and gave instructions for his and his family's salvation.

It had never rained on the earth; a fine mist would come and go to provide moisture for all vegetation to flourish, but it was never water falling from the sky. The only water anyone had ever seen was found in the lakes, rivers and oceans. God spoke to Noah, telling him that He would destroy all life on the Earth with a great flood of water. Yet, He would spare Noah and his family – establishing a covenant with them.

Specific instructions were given to Noah, and he discussed God's plan with his family. He purchased wood, crafted scaffolding and began to build the biggest boat anyone had ever seen – away from any body of water. As the project grew, it attracted attention throughout the land, inducing laughter from those who saw it. Even Noah's sons and their wives questioned if Noah had truly heard these instructions from God.

Whispers soon became outright derogatory shouts and taunting as all around him he heard, "What is he building? Why is he building it that big? How will he get it to the water? Has Noah lost his mind? Who is he that he thinks God spoke to him?"

Noah was not swayed in his focus and continued to work diligently, month after month, following every detail of God's blueprint. Eventually the time arrived for him to begin to gather pairs of every creature to bring into the ark. This endeavor stirred the critics again, yet Noah and his family were not deterred. Every creature arrived and was tucked away for what was to come – all according to the plan of God.

The building was complete, the animals were loaded and all preparations were finalized. Noah and his family stepped off the Earth for the last time as they moved up the plank into the ark. The hand of God reached down, lifted the huge door and sealed the opening as those on board breathed one last breath of what was. The Earth and life they had known would soon be gone, what was ahead of them was uncertain.

There had been no repentance from the wickedness that had consumed the world, so it would now be engulfed with water – every stain washed away, and everything destroyed.

The sound was deafening as the waters began to fall, pounding down upon the wood that surrounded them. The ark began to move, listing back and forth as it was lifted by the waters. For forty days the water came from below and above, swaying the huge vessel as it moved. All life outside of the ark died in the wake of the waters.

Noah and his family remained isolated within the ark for nearly a year after the rain stopped. All that was left of mankind was sheltered within this boat – they would be God's new beginning.

God established His covenant with Noah: a promise that He would never again eradicate life from the Earth with a flood. His promise was bound with a gift, topped with a bow – a rainbow – that would be seen from the clouds. A symbolic reminder of a promise to be fulfilled.

This symbol is a reminder of God's love and faithfulness. It is also a reminder of the promise of salvation – a promise completed at the cross of Jesus Christ, where all of our sin was washed away by the shedding of His blood, making all things new.

(Enjoy reading the whole story in Genesis 6 - 9)

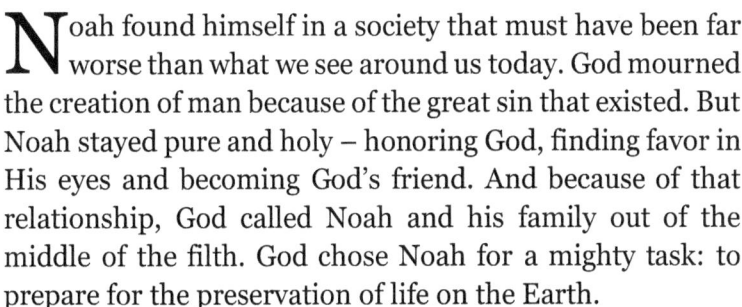

Noah found himself in a society that must have been far worse than what we see around us today. God mourned the creation of man because of the great sin that existed. But Noah stayed pure and holy – honoring God, finding favor in His eyes and becoming God's friend. And because of that relationship, God called Noah and his family out of the middle of the filth. God chose Noah for a mighty task: to prepare for the preservation of life on the Earth.

As we look at today's society and see the lawlessness, violence, sexual exploitations and every unimaginable perversion, we think *it can't get much worse.* We are inundated from every arena with behaviors that are contrary to God's desire.

Do you often feel uncomfortable in situations, exiting quickly to avoid exposure to what you know is wrong? You are not alone. We are called to be holy – I know that sounds like an archaic thought – but sin and holy do not go together.

Noah's stand against the sinful society he lived in became extremely obvious when God gave him the instruction to build an ark. Imagine the ridicule, the laughter and the spread of "fake news" that surrounded him. I'm sure that even his own children and their spouses may have had a few questions as the project grew astronomically.

When we stand on God's instructions for our lives, it may go against other's thoughts, opinions and beliefs; it has never been promised that choosing to follow His directions would be easy. Faith is what will stir you to accept the assignment God has placed before you and to believe that God can do it. Noah listened, believed and moved out to accomplish a great task, standing on the faith that God declared what was to be done and that He would do it. Noah just picked up the hammer and went to work.

God chose to prepare the Earth for a *new beginning* and Noah and his family were given the privilege to be part of the process. What was required was a pure and holy life that was free from the world's entanglements, a listening and obedient heart, and a willingness to be separated. Noah's love, trust and friendship with God were the keys to a promised new life – a life free from the surrounding chaos.

God chose Noah, His friend, and desired to use him for His perfectly-timed salvation of mankind. Though much was required, much was promised. Closed inside the ark, that long, treacherous year must have been formidable to every relationship that was housed within it. Yet they persevered, and, in the end, accomplished God's plan of a new beginning for all life.

As Noah disembarked the ark, a rainbow shined across the sky to signal a covenant of love for Noah – a promise of God's faithfulness, both then and now.

Summary thought:

When we see a rainbow, our hope is stirred; joy crosses our face and peace settles over all that chaos shouts into our life – this promise of the rainbow is a symbol of the great love that our Lord has for each of us.

If you find yourself hidden in the bottom of a dark place, isolated from all that is familiar, remember that He has a perfect time for you to come out of this hidden place. He has a planned time when you will shine and your new life will begin.

As you hold on to faith, remember that He always has the best for you; persevere and fight forward into the new place He is establishing for you – His time to open the door is always perfect.

Keep your heart clean and holy before the Lord; listen intently, obey immediately and pick up the hammer when He calls you to go to work.

1 Pet. 1:15-16 but as he who called you is holy, you also be holy in all your conduct, since it is written, "You shall be holy, for I am holy."

Prov. 23:12 Apply your heart to instruction and your ear to words of knowledge.

Gen. 9:13-17 I have set my bow in the cloud, and it shall be a sign of the covenant between me and the earth. When I bring clouds over the earth and the bow is seen in the clouds, I will remember my covenant that is between me and you and every living creature of all flesh. And the waters shall never again become a flood to destroy all flesh. When the bow is in the clouds, I will see it and remember the everlasting covenant between God and every living creature of all flesh that is on the earth." God said to Noah, "This is the sign of the covenant that I have established between me and all flesh that is on the earth."

Personal Insights:
_____
_____
_____
_____
_____
_____

H: How Does this Apply to Me?
_____
_____
_____
_____

O: Observations:
_____
_____
_____
_____

P: Personal Prayer:
_____
_____
_____
_____

E: Expression Through My Life (Action Step):
_____
_____
_____
_____

Resentful to Merciful

As a prophet of the living God, Jonah knew that when God spoke, He required obedience. But one day the words God spoke to him, "Go to Nineveh and declare their evil that they might repent," brought a different response.

Nineveh was a large city – it was a three-day walk from one side to the other. Filled with detestable sin and a myriad of gods, Jonah believed this place was unsalvageable and he did not want to go. So, he ran. He ran from the presence of God and in the exact opposite direction – away from Nineveh.

Jonah went as far as he could, right up to the edge of the sea, and continued to run. He bought passage on a ship to take him further away and immediately went to the bottom of the ship to hide. He was still hoping he could run and hide from the presence of God.

The Lord stirred up a viciously-strong tempest that threatened to pull the ship, its crew and all its cargo to the bottom of the sea. Fear gripped the crew. They had not seen this type of storm in nature's normal course, so their assumption was that this storm had come upon them because of someone's sin. They drew lots to determine the culprit and the lot fell on Jonah.

Jonah admitted his folly and told the men to throw him into the sea so they would not die. As the waves crashed over the ship, the crew did as Jonah requested and threw him overboard into the churning depths. Immediately the winds stopped, and the men believed in and feared Jonah's God.

Jonah sank into the depths of the sea. Darkness suddenly surrounded him as he was swallowed by a huge fish. His mind swirled with thoughts of the reality that this would be how his life would end. His disobedience to God had landed him in this position – yet even here he could not run from the presence of the Lord.

Hidden in the belly of the fish – wet, cold and hungry – Jonah called out to God. For three silent days in the darkness he prayed and repented. Day after day passed. Finally, on the third day, the Lord spoke to the fish and Jonah was vomited out onto the dry land. And then God spoke to Jonah again, "Arise, go to Nineveh, that great city, and call out against it the message that I tell you" (Jonah 3:2).

He obeyed God and went to Nineveh, preaching throughout the city and speaking against their sin. He warned them that within forty days God's destruction was eminent and called them to repent: their time was running out.

The word spread and the people believed God. The king called for a time of fasting and prayer, hoping that God would honor their repentance and relent from His anger against them. "Just maybe, God will forgive us, that we won't perish," declared the king.

The Lord did hear. He saw the heart of repentance that engulfed the city and forgave them, and He did not bring destruction.

Jonah did not agree; he was angry at the Lord's show of compassion on this sinful city. He was quick to forget the forgiveness of the Lord – that same forgiveness that was poured out to him because of his recent disobedience. But God loved Jonah, and continued to speak, instruct and reveal His compassionate nature to him. And in the end, Jonah's resentful heart was adjusted, becoming one of mercy.

(Enjoy reading the whole story in Jonah 1-4)

As a mother I have found myself saying the dreaded, "Because I said so!" My expectation is that my children will listen and obey. But as they grow old enough to make their own decisions, they often think they know better ways – which repeatedly results in natural consequences. It is hard to watch those ramifications occur, but it is the only way that they will learn.

Jonah heard God, but chose to do what he thought was better. Judging those who God hoped to redeem, Jonah chose to ignore – in fact, run away from – God's directive. He prejudged Nineveh as unredeemable. God's natural consequences were rather drastic, but they got Jonah's attention. We better listen when God says, "Because I said so!"

Most of us hear this story and think, "Wow, if God spoke to me, I wouldn't disobey. I would never judge someone unforgivable." But yet – we do. We are told throughout the Word of God about God's grace and forgiveness for us, and we believe and receive it. However, somewhere between the personal acceptance and the willingness to declare it to others, we decide that they don't deserve it and are unredeemable: so, we run! Your consequences might not be like Jonah, finding yourself in the belly of a huge fish, but the devastation may still land you in a place where God needs to *change your mind*.

I can only imagine the stench and the cold, wet, darkness that surrounded Jonah for three days as he contemplated his fate. He called out to God – the God he had been running from – but he heard no response. God kept Jonah hidden deep, away from His presence, allowing his own need for forgiveness to generate a true repentance – a true changed mind.

Out of desperation, his mind did change, and he did as God requested. But it still took more time in the presence of God to turn his heart from one of judgement into one of mercy.

God's heart for Nineveh was filled with desire that they would turn back to Him. He was willing to forgive them and He wanted to use Jonah to share this great message. But God had to shape the outcome around a man who had a hard heart, hiding him in a very uncomfortable situation to prepare him for the assignment that God had asked him to perform.

Believing and understanding the grace of God – the free gift of forgiveness – belongs to every person who accepts Jesus as their personal Lord and Savior. With that understanding, we begin a walk of freedom that must extent to those around us. Walking in mercy is not an easy walk – but running away as you carry the burden of judgment and unforgiveness only brings about unpleasant consequences.

If Jesus is whispering, *"Because I said so,"* to your heart, it's as simple as turning to Him and saying, "Please forgive me Lord." Don't run away – run into His arms, they are always ready to welcome you into His presence.

Summary thought:

The Lord's love and forgiveness is available to everyone – there is not one unsalvageable individual. His desire is to free you from judgment, to bring freedom into your life and to use you to break the chains that others are carrying. Shake off the judgment that whispers in your ear and run to the foot of the Cross. Allow the Holy Spirit to change a broken, hurt, resentful spirit into one full and overflowing with the grace and love of Jesus.

Step into a time of preparation – a time where He desires to change your mind and adjust your heart. He will fill you with His mercy for others. Trust that now is the time – His perfect time to use you – to release the captives as you speak love into the lives around you.

Luke 1:16-17 And he will turn many of the children of Israel to the Lord their God, and he will go before him in the spirit and power of Elijah, to turn the hearts of the fathers to the children, and the disobedient to the wisdom of the just, to make ready for the Lord a people prepared."

Rom. 12:3 For by the grace given to me I say to everyone among you not to think of himself more highly than he ought to think, but to think with sober judgment, each according to the measure of faith that God has assigned.

Rom. 14:13 Therefore let us not pass judgment on one another any longer, but rather decide never to put a stumbling block or hindrance in the way of a brother.

Personal Insights:
_____
_____
_____
_____
_____
_____

H: How Does this Apply to Me?
_____
_____
_____
_____

O: Observations:
_____
_____
_____
_____

P: Personal Prayer:
_____
_____
_____
_____

E: Expression Through My Life (Action Step):
_____
_____
_____
_____

Chapter 8

Hidden to Come Forth

Rom. 15:13 May the God of hope fill you with joy and peace in believing, so that by the power of the Holy Spirit you may abound in hope.

Hidden to Come Forth

Stories of Victory from Hidden Places

Hope tells us that God always has the best waiting for us and that there is a great future available and coming. When that hope is tested, something remarkable happens: it changes from mere agreement into belief. In this place, you now can say, "Yes, Lord." The presence of a deep reliance and confidence in Jesus Christ now resides within you – He is the one that you know you can trust and have set your hope and belief in. Somewhere in that testing, in the hidden waiting process, your belief will shift into faith. Faith tells us that all we have been hoping for is available and here for us now. It is in the midst of the greatest difficulties that we find faith – a living and active faith – that will allow us to confidently step into the fiery furnace or the lion's den, knowing God is in control, no matter the outcome.

With this faith, we find God's preparation as He turns dark times into explosions of power and glory that declare His transformational ability to bring forth that which was thought to be dead. This explosive transformational power is found in many biblical stories, some, where death turned into resurrected life, a fiery furnace expelled the unscathed, hungry lions turned from their prey and forty days of prayer and fasting ushered in the arrival of God's power and presence to send forth the Gospel into the world. Each miracle was hinged on unshakable faith.

God's ultimate plan is your transformation! He prepares you to be called forth into an assignment that only you can complete.

Knowing who your hope is in, believing that you can trust Him and stepping into a living and active faith are all found as preparation takes place. Yield to His plan and timing as you rest into the waiting process, and expect your patience to bring forth fruit. Your hope will begin to stir, belief will rise and soon, your faith will be ignited. You are being prepared and made ready for Jesus to call your name to "come forth." Just say, "Yes, Lord," and move forward.

From Death to Life

The fever raged within Lazarus as he gave into its heat, and took to his bed. As their brother's illness drastically weakened him, Martha and Mary's concern heightened. With determination, they decided, "Let's send for Jesus. If He comes, surely He will heal him."

The word was quickly sent, encouraging Jesus to come and help the friend that He loved. But when Jesus heard the request he said, "This illness does not lead to death. It is for the glory of God, so that the Son of God may be glorified through it" (John 11:4). Jesus waited two more days before heading to Bethany.

When the third day arrived, Jesus told his disciples of His plans and His need to visit His friends in Bethany. Concern and confusion filtered through the group; going back to where the Jews were seeking to stone Jesus, just to visit a friend who was "sleeping" made little sense, until Jesus spoke plainly, "Lazarus has died, and for your sake I am glad that I was not there, so that you may believe. But let us go to him" (John 11:14-15).

The sun had crossed the sky as Jesus neared Bethany, and the midday heat beat down on them. The news of His approach was whispered through the crowd that had gathered to mourn and console Martha and Mary. Martha immediately went out to meet Him, while Mary stayed grieving at home.

Martha's grief was evident as she greeted Jesus. She said to Jesus, "Lord, if you had been here, my brother would not have died" (John 11:21).

The inconsolable pain in her eyes was evident, yet Jesus assured her of his resurrection. Her hope tilted toward faith as one statement from Jesus was spoken.

Jesus said to her, "I am the resurrection and the life. Whoever believes in me, though he die, yet shall he live, and everyone who lives and believes in me shall never die. Do you believe this?" (John 11:25-26).

With an explosion of faith, Martha declared that she did believe. She knew that He was the Christ, the Son of God and the One who was to come into the world. And with a renewed faith, she quickly returned home, whispering to Mary, "The Teacher is here and is calling for you." Mary swiftly went out to meet Jesus, and the grieving houseful of friends followed her.

Seeing Jesus, Mary fell to the ground, grief overwhelming her as she wept. Questions, broken expectations and hurt overflowed from Mary, as well as those around her. Jesus wept, being grieved by the hopelessness he saw within their eyes. He turned and requested they take him to the tomb where Lazarus had been laid.

The tomb had been sealed and Lazarus had been laid within it four days earlier. Aghast at Jesus' request for the stone to be removed, the crowd waited breathlessly.

Jesus said, "Did I not tell you that if you believed you would see the glory of God?" (John 11:40).

The stone was slowly rolled away from the cave's opening as Jesus lifted His eyes and prayed. With one loud voice He shouted, "Lazarus, come forth!"

Shock rippled through the crowd at this audacious act. Tension rose and anticipation grew minute by minute. A slight rustling could be heard coming from within the cave and a movement was soon observed, as something began to happen. Questions swirled breathlessly through the minds of those waiting and watching, "Is it the sun in our eyes? Maybe it is a mirage from the heat?" But before them, a man bound and wrapped with grave clothes was standing upright in front of the entrance to the tomb.

Those questions and doubts suddenly turned from stunned observation into exuberant, celebratory shouts of joy, as Jesus said, "Unbind him and let him go."

Jesus raised Lazarus from death to life! On that day, the power and glory of God was shown when three words were spoken: "Lazarus, come forth." With those words, Jesus gave the world a glimpse of His authority over death.

(Enjoy reading the whole story in John 11)

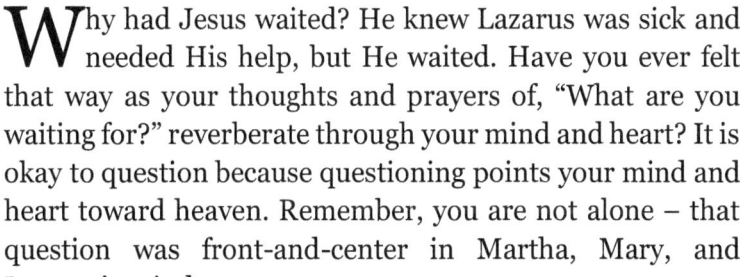

Why had Jesus waited? He knew Lazarus was sick and needed His help, but He waited. Have you ever felt that way as your thoughts and prayers of, "What are you waiting for?" reverberate through your mind and heart? It is okay to question because questioning points your mind and heart toward heaven. Remember, you are not alone – that question was front-and-center in Martha, Mary, and Lazarus's minds, too.

Our expectations are much like Lazarus' sisters. If we ask, we expect Him to come and help – but when the answer is "no" or "wait," disappointment settles over us, shrouding us with grief and confusion. Each time we encounter a time of waiting, something occurs within our hearts: either we become hardened or we yield. Ultimately, we have no choice in the matter but to wait – that is where hope and belief are formed.

Remember Martha from early in the gospel? She was the sister that was so busy, anxious, worried and distracted about getting everything done, while her sister sat at Jesus' feet. Now we find that same Martha being the first to run to meet Jesus and the first to believe His declaration of "I am the resurrection and the life." Somewhere between these two stories she found faith – a faith that had transformed from hope into belief, then ended in faith. She didn't become offended by Jesus rebuke, but instead she yielded – and the change is obvious.

The <u>waiting</u> is all part of the process. The glory of God always shows up in our lives at the right time – His time. It may not be what we *think* is the right time – in fact, it usually does not *feel* like the right time. It might be as you stand before the stone-sealed tomb of a hope of your own, or it might be as you've been crying out to God for His help and the answer has not come. Trust Him in this difficult place, I know that that may seem easier said than done, but when you have no strength left, reach out to Him and He will meet you. Place your hope not on what you see but on what you *don't* see – because His presence is always sure and His promises will never fail you; His love overflows around you, His glory will arrive and cover you as peace arrives. Somewhere during your <u>waiting process</u>, your hope will change into belief and bloom into a living and active faith.

Remember, Jesus waited so the glory of God would be revealed. It is okay to wait and find refuge under His wings. Yield and know that at His timing He will shout, "Come forth," and freedom will erupt in your life. His plan is always for the best for you and for His glory to be revealed in you.

Summary thought:

Jesus waited for multiple purposes:

1) The rabbinical law taught that for three days a soul hovered around the earth realm, but on the fourth day it left for eternity. When Jesus called Lazarus to "come forth" – giving back life where death had reigned – they knew that he was raised back from eternity.

2) This was a precursor of what He was preparing to do: to die and rise again. This was an example of the miracle of the Cross to those who believe – He delivered us out of the tomb, just as He did Lazarus. This resurrection is a glimpse of the authority He has over death.

3) Waiting changed hope into belief, then belief shifted into faith when Jesus asked Martha if she believed that He was the resurrection and the life. Faith ignited the ability for miracles to occur.

Jesus still asks, "Do you believe?" Believing that Jesus is the Christ and that He died for you – paying your debt in full, releasing you from sin's bondage on your life and giving you freedom and life eternal – requires a simple, "Yes, Lord." Just as Jesus called Lazarus to "come forth," He calls for you to also. Your response changes mere knowledge to belief. This belief erupts into a sure confidence and reliance on Him alone.

Heb. 11:1 Now faith is the assurance of things hoped for, the conviction of things not seen.

John 14:1 Don't worry or surrender to your fear. For you've believed in God, now trust and believe in me also. (TPT)

2 Cor. 4:16-18 So no wonder we don't give up. For even though our outer person gradually wears out, our inner being is renewed every single day. We view our slight, short-lived troubles in the light of eternity. We see our difficulties as the substance that produces for us an eternal, weighty glory far beyond all comparison, because we don't focus our attention on what is seen but on what is unseen. For what is seen is temporary, but the unseen realm is eternal. (TPT)

Personal Insights:
_____
_____
_____
_____
_____
_____

H: How Does this Apply to Me?
_____
_____
_____
_____

O: Observations:
_____
_____
_____
_____

P: Personal Prayer:
_____
_____
_____
_____

E: Expression Through My Life (Action Step):
_____
_____
_____
_____

Not a Hair Singed

*A*ctivity reverberated through the kingdom as gold was heated and poured, frames and scaffolding were built and artisans crafted the growing image. The people looked on with excitement as the ninety-foot image of the king took shape and reached toward the sky – at least, most of the people did.

The king's newly-announced decree required all individuals to fall down and worship the image whenever music was heard. But in the eyes of the Jews, God's law was a non-negotiable law, and this decree was not going to be part of their lives. Only the living God – the God of Israel – was worthy of worship and praise.

Shadrach, Meshach and Abednego, three young Jewish men, had just been appointed by Daniel to take care of the king's affairs in the Babylon province. As the excitement over the construction of the golden image grew throughout the kingdom, concern surged within these three young men. The king's decree pronounced death in the fiery furnace to anyone who refused to bow before the king's image.

The dreaded day came: as the horn was blown, people fell to their knees to worship the image – yet three young Jewish men chose to stand. Their knees would only bow to the King of kings – the living God – Yahweh. The defiance of Shadrach, Meshach and Abednego quickly brought malicious accusers and swift retaliation found them before the king.

The king's rage erupted when the men's adamant disobedience continued. He questioned them and gave them one more chance to fall down and worship at his feet. He said, "Now if you are ready when you hear the sound of the horn, pipe, lyre, trigon, harp, bagpipe, and every kind of music, to fall down and worship the image that I have made, well and good. But if you do not worship you shall immediately be cast into a burning fiery furnace. And who is the god who will deliver you out of my hands?" (Dan. 3:15).

Without hesitation they responded, "If this be so, our God whom we serve is able to deliver us from the burning fiery furnace, and he will deliver us out of your hand, O king. But if not, be it known to you, O king, that we will not serve your gods or worship the golden image that you have set up" (Dan. 3:17-18). Without any jury's input, death was the verdict handed down to the disobedient.

The fire blazed as instruction was given to heat the furnace seven times hotter than normal. The king was determined that this disobedience would not be tolerated, and that today an example would be made before the people of his kingdom: they would worship him and him only, or they would die. Quickly, Shadrach, Meshach and Abednego were tightly bound, with every garment they owned, and thrown into the furnace.

They could feel the heat long before they reached the opening, but they walked forward carrying a peace that they could not understand. Hope in the living God had been solidified in their lives since childhood, and today a spark erupted – a spark of deep faith – that would carry them into this fire. They trusted that their God was in control, no matter what the outcome.

The power of the fire's ferocious appetite permeated the environment. The king watched as it engulfed the three lawbreakers, but also watched the soldiers who had accomplished the job be turned to ash before they could move away from the fire's fury.

Astonished by what appeared to be occurring within the flames, the king quickly rose, drawing close to the opening in order to be sure. "Did we not cast three men in? How can this be? I see four unbound men walking in the midst of the flames – unharmed!" Reality slowly settled over his mind and he called out to them, "Shadrach, Meshach and Abednego, servants of the Most High God, come out and come here!"

All the officials of the kingdom who had gathered to see justice doled out now stood in shock, as the three young men stepped out of the furnace. The fire had not had any power over their bodies; their clothes were not harmed, not a hair on their heads was singed and no smell of fire lingered on them.

Nebuchadnezzar, the king, said, "Blessed be the God of Shadrach, Meshach, and Abednego, who has sent his angel and delivered his servants, who trusted in him, and set aside the king's command, and yielded up their bodies rather than serve and worship any god except their own God" (Dan. 3:28). And with that declaration, the young Jewish men were promoted as officials of the kingdom, where they faithfully served only their God – the true living God – and found favor throughout the Babylon province.

(Enjoy reading the whole story in Dan. 3)

Your faith and integrity matter. They are seen by others, even if you don't *think* they are – because people are watching. Have you read this story and thought *it is just a story?*

Living in the United States, we take for granted our rights to believe and worship as we desire. But it is a gift that our forefathers fought hard for; throughout the world, people are still sacrificing their lives to stand on their faith.

Shadrach, Meshach and Abednego chose to believe in the living God. The hope they carried from childhood suddenly came to an abrupt wall – a choice had to be made. Would they believe what they had learned, or would they "go with the flow" with the majority of their society and just do what the government was asking them to do?

Many make that choice today, both around the world and here in the United States. Our hope in Jesus Christ begins in our learned knowledge; what we have heard, read and been taught stirs hope, an optimistic attitude and an understanding that there is something better to come. From that internal *knowing*, hope begins to speak into our hearts, "The *best* is on its way."

Hope constantly pulses deep within us, telling us that we are loved and going to make it. Hope is that which moves us to a place where belief steps up and allows us to overcome our obstacles with a newfound, confident faith that is unshakable.

When we come to the stretching times – the hidden times of decision – when we are required to step past that hope and say, "Yes, that is truth," we can stand on an active, living faith, no matter the cost. This is where Shadrach, Meshach and Abednego found themselves, and their lives depended on their decision.

Making a stand for what you know is truth is always hard and consequences must be paid, but integrity within the core of your being will always win. Shadrach, Meshach and Abednego found their hope ignited into a flaming faith as they chose to believe and proclaim Yahweh – the only true and living God – before the king, his officials and a nation.

When faith is ignited, miracles enter. Shadrach, Meshach and Abednego entered the flames with a peace that only comes from Christ. They met Jesus within the flames where they were surrounded by His presence and were protected and delivered out of the fire with not a single hair singed. This miracle showed the great power that resides in our God. That power was stirred through the faith of His people.

They were hidden within that fire, yet were not burned or harmed in any way. They *came forth*, showing a nation the power of God – the living God. It is our turn to allow the fire that surrounds us to ignite our faith and to stand up and declare the truth – the gospel of Jesus Christ. Let's trust in the delivering power of Christ as we pour out the love, forgiveness, freedom and healing of Jesus over a broken and hurting nation.

Summary thought:

Everyone needs to know, deep within, who they believe in and who they were created to be. From birth, those two questions begin to surge within you. The answers are found throughout your life, usually in the middle of your own fiery furnace. How you respond creates a catalyst where you find hope. This newfound hope stirs a confident belief and ignites faith which will release the explosive power of God – and miracles can follow. This becomes a lifestyle directed by the Holy Spirit as you move out of the fire into a hurting nation.

Choose to yield your life into the hand of God as you walk through the hidden place of your own fiery furnace and allow His transformation to occur. When He calls, "Come forth," you will come out with garments untouched: pure, holy and clean through the blood of Jesus Christ.

Heb. 11:6 And without faith living within us it would be impossible to please God. For we come to God in faith knowing that he is real and that he rewards the faith of those who give all their passion and strength into seeking him. (TPT)

Phil. 4:7 And the peace of God, which surpasses all understanding, will guard your hearts and your minds in Christ Jesus.

Matt. 4:10 Then Jesus said to him, "Be gone, Satan! For it is written, "'You shall worship the Lord your God and him only shall you serve.'"

Personal Insights:
___

H: How Does this Apply to Me?
___

O: Observations:
___

P: Personal Prayer:
___

E: Expression Through My Life (Action Step):
___

Out of the Lion's Mouths

A man, full of wisdom and understanding, who faithfully and whole-heartedly served the God of Israel, found favor before the king: his name was Daniel. He gained repeated acknowledgement as he interpreted the king's dreams, and he built a reputation of honor with both the king and his high officials.

When Daniel was given greater responsibility, word began to circulate that the king was contemplating setting him over the entire kingdom and jealousy began to whisper in the ears of those same high officials. They determined amongst themselves to find grounds to discredit Daniel, but his high level of integrity prevented any hole in his credibility. Frustrated with every attempt, they considered another plot. Then these men said, "We shall not find any ground for complaint against this Daniel unless we find it in connection with the law of his God" (Dan. 6:5).

Conspiring together, they contrived a trap that would surely rid them of this "goodie-goodie" Israelite, once and for all. Preying on the king's vanity and need for adulation, they requested an injunction be declared for thirty days: that no one could make a petition to any god or man except the king, and that anyone who did so would be thrown into the lion's den. The king pridefully agreed, signing it into law.

Daniel knew of this document but his faithfulness to God was unwavering. Undeterred in his worship, he knelt down three times a day as he lifted up prayers and supplications before His God.

The trap worked just as the officials had hoped, immediately catching Daniel as he brought petitions to his God. Like children running to "tattle," they encircled the king asking, "O king! Did you not sign an injunction, that anyone who makes petition to any god or man within thirty days except to you, O king, shall be cast into the den of lions?"

This was a truth that both the officials and the king knew could not be changed; the declaration was irrevocable and would have to stand. The king's heart grew heavy, as he listened to the officials declare Daniel's guilt in breaking the law. He was distressed and searched until sundown to find an answer that would allow the rescue of Daniel from what he had declared, but the officials would not be silenced. They demanded that the law be followed.

With great sadness, the king said to Daniel, "May your God, whom you serve continually, deliver you," and he commanded that Daniel be thrown into the lion's den. The king returned to the palace where he spent a sleepless night fasting, waiting and hoping that Daniel's God might rescue him.

At daybreak, the king made his way to the den of lions with great urgency and cried out in anguish, "O Daniel, servant of the living God, has your God, whom you serve continually, been able to deliver you from the lions?"
(Dan. 6:20b). With heart pounding, he waited in hopes of hearing some sound.

From the pit, Daniel responded, "My God sent his angel and shut the lions' mouths, and they have not harmed me, because I was found blameless before him; and also, before you, O king, I have done no harm" (Dan. 6:22).

Daniel was lifted from the pit, and not a scratch was found on him. He was replaced with the malicious officials that had tricked the king into the decree, and the sound of the hungry lions' satisfaction was immediately heard.

The hope that the king had voiced to heaven throughout that long, dark night flourished into a deep faith and acknowledgment of Daniel's God – the living God. A decree was announced throughout the land that the people were to worship the God of Daniel.

(Enjoy reading the whole story in Dan. 6)

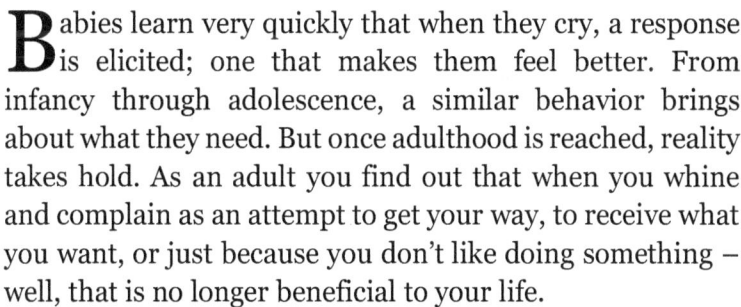

Babies learn very quickly that when they cry, a response is elicited; one that makes them feel better. From infancy through adolescence, a similar behavior brings about what they need. But once adulthood is reached, reality takes hold. As an adult you find out that when you whine and complain as an attempt to get your way, to receive what you want, or just because you don't like doing something – well, that is no longer beneficial to your life.

That sounds like a *no-brainer* – but stop and think about how you reach out to talk to God. Do you pray in faith or do you whine, beg and complain? *Now wait, what does this have to do with the story of Daniel and the lion's den?* A lot! Let's think about what got him there.

Daniel was a man of faith, a man of integrity, a man of understanding and wisdom and a man highly favored by the Lord. He was faithful to God and he knew Him intimately, taking time every day to pray – in fact, three times each day he brought prayers, supplications and intercession before God. These were not times of whining, complaining or begging, but instead times of thanksgiving and bringing humble requests for help, wisdom and understanding, as well as intercession for the needs of others. His prayer life became the target of attack by others who wanted his position. It was the only thing they would have a chance to manipulate and use to take him down – or so they *thought*.

When you find yourself struggling with trouble, sickness or a great loss, how do you respond? Do you look first to God? Or do you look first for help elsewhere, such as online, "dumping" on a friend, social media, or to some other unhealthy diversions? Daniel ran to the feet of his Lord, and that is where our hope is also found. It is at the feet of Jesus where you will find what you need to get through the tough times.

Daniel loved God above all else, and his trust in God's faithfulness carried him into the lion's pit. That faith continued to carry him through a long, dark night as he heard the rustle of movement and felt the hot breath of lions as they circled him. And that same faith walked him out of the lion's den at dawn – unharmed. God protected him as he silently waited in this frightening place. He was hidden away, with teeth chomping at him, yet God did not forget him – He stood right there beside him.

You might feel the hot breath of destruction over your life right now, but have faith that God is with you in the midst of your struggle. Look into the face of your Lord and trust that He *has your back*. Go to the feet of Jesus and, with a humble heart, lay your requests before Him – He knows everything you are walking through.

Just like Daniel, your time of hiding will come to an end and you will be called to *come forth*. Your job is to trust Him and pray with faith for His plan in your life; pray in faith as you wait in the midst of the lions, knowing His protection surrounds you.

And remember, just as it was for Daniel, those around you are watching how you respond. The king and the nation turned to worship Daniel's God – the living God – not only because of the miraculous protection and redemption he experienced in the lion's den, but also the faith and integrity he walked in as he walked through the process. Trust in God's plan and purpose for your life, even now, in the hidden place, as you trust and wait for His deliverance.

Summary thought:

The presence of God walks with you through the most difficult times of your life. Your faith in His faithfulness anchors you, carrying you through the storm. Don't allow the turmoil of life to cause you to falter or give up on your hope. Fight forward in faith – He will call you out of the hidden dark times and you will find that He was with you every step of the way.

Matt. 22:37 And he said to him, "You shall love the Lord your God with all your heart and with all your soul and with all your mind."

Ps. 91:14-15 For here is what the Lord has spoken to me: "Because you have delighted in me as my great lover, I will greatly protect you. I will set you in a high place, safe and secure before my face. I will answer your cry for help every time you pray, and you will find and feel my presence even in your time of pressure and trouble. I will be your glorious hero and give you a feast. (TPT)

2 Cor. 7:10 For godly grief produces a repentance that leads to salvation without regret, whereas worldly grief produces death.

Personal Insights:
_____
_____
_____
_____
_____
_____
_____

H: How Does this Apply to Me?
_____
_____
_____
_____

O: Observations:
_____
_____
_____
_____

P: Personal Prayer:
_____
_____
_____
_____

E: Expression Through My Life (Action Step):
_____
_____
_____
_____

Fire in the Upper Room

For thirty-nine days they had waited in this upper room, praying and fasting, waiting for the promise of something – a gift of some sort – a gift that Jesus had said would come. The first two weeks they grieved their great loss; holding one another, crying together and reminiscing over the last three years. Slowly the cloud over their hearts lifted, and for a couple of weeks a time of determined prayer and fasting followed. But over the last few days, the group of 120 began to struggle. Doubt nibbled at their resolve as anticipation of truly receiving a gift from heaven began to fade away.

The need to take care of a few leadership details and preparation for Pentecost distracted them from the monotonous "waiting game" that was being played out day after day. As the day of Pentecost arrived, all 120 of the group were together, and with one heart and mind they lifted their voices in prayer and praise.

Suddenly, the growing sound of wild, rushing wind surrounded them, filling the whole house and silencing their prayers. With pounding hearts, they were intently attuned to the presence of the supernatural visit that was beginning. Flames of fire arrived, materializing before their eyes. As if it were alive, it began to move and divide, sitting upon each person as the promised gift that Jesus had spoken of filled them with unimaginable joy. The arrival of the presence of God through the third person of the trinity – Holy Spirit – brought a power, boldness and new language of utterances, unknown to those who spoke them.

The bewildering sounds that originated in the upper room astonished those throughout Jerusalem, drawing devote men from every nation to the building. Each one was hearing these people – many who were simple, uneducated fishermen – now speaking in their own languages, declaring the mighty works of God.

With great boldness, the disciples came out! Coming forth from their grief, pain, fear, and doubt, they came into a new mission, the mission that Jesus had given them. For Jesus had said, "Go into all the world and proclaim the gospel to all of mankind, making disciples and baptizing them in the name of the Father and of the Son and of the Holy Spirit."

The power that they received on the day of Pentecost was the gift Jesus had promised – a gift that infused simple, uneducated men with faith and boldness to speak forth the truth of Christ. The Holy Spirit's arrival on that day forever changed these fishermen. This gift from heaven filled them with hope and faith to come out of hiding and complete the commission Jesus had set for them to complete, releasing the Gospel to the world.

(Enjoy reading the whole story in Acts 2)

Waiting is a discipline that no one likes; it requires that formidable word: "patience." The followers of Jesus had been gathered together, waiting for nearly forty days – I bet patience was growing thin in the house.

Ultimately, waiting does end. It is the waiting *process* that provides transformation. This truth surrounds us – bulbs and seeds explode with new growth and eggs hatch with new life. Your wedding day eventually dawns, the baby arrives *right on time* and retirement suddenly overtakes you; each event requires waiting, patience and transformation.

The *waiting process* would teach the disciples *how* to wait for God's timing, as it also required them to walk in patience and be diligent in prayer and fasting. Unknown to them, these disciplines would soon be crucial when the gift that Jesus had promised was received. With an encounter of explosive boldness and power, the gift of the Holy Spirit's living presence showed up in the upper room. This long-awaited gift surprised everyone, as transformation became evident – sending the disciples to the street, declaring the gospel.

The gift received in the upper room is a gift that Jesus has available to every believer. The active, living presence of the Holy Spirit will be with you every day and He is your continual comforter. He brings wisdom and understanding when confusion reigns, He brings peace when turmoil threatens to pull you under, and He pours boldness, faith and power through you as you step out speaking, laying hands on the sick and bringing the freedom of Christ to others.

Transformation begins when you receive the free gift of eternal salvation through the blood that Jesus shed on the Cross for all of mankind. The indwelling, living presence of the Holy Spirit is a gift that allows a continual transformation and growth in your life and the lives of those you encounter.

This same transformation made simple, uneducated fishermen into fishers of men and it is the same transformational power that now resides in you.

Summary thought:

If you are in a waiting period, take this time to learn the *waiting process* – allow it to work the needed disciplines within you; they will be required when He calls you to "come forth." As you wait at His feet you will be prepared for what is ahead. Don't give up. Stay filled with hope – the joy that He has set before you will require times of transformation that will always start with patience and waiting. Rest in the *process* and expect His release to come, thrusting you forward into new growth, new life and new joy.

Matt. 28:18-20 Then Jesus came close to them and said, "All the authority of the universe has been given to me. Now go *in my authority* and make disciples of all nations, baptizing them in the name of the Father, the Son, and the Holy Spirit. And teach them to faithfully follow all that I have commanded you. And never forget that I am with you every day, even to the completion of this age." (TPT)

Ps. 27:14 Here's what I've learned through it all: Don't give up; don't be impatient; be entwined as one with the Lord. Be brave and courageous, and never lose hope. Yes, keep on waiting—for he will never disappoint you! (TPT)

Rom. 15:13 Now may God, the inspiration and fountain of hope, fill you to overflowing with uncontainable joy and perfect peace as you trust in him. And may the power of the Holy Spirit continually surround your life with his super-abundance until you radiate with hope! (TPT)

Personal Insights:
_____
_____
_____
_____
_____
_____

H: How Does this Apply to Me?
_____
_____
_____
_____

O: Observations:
_____
_____
_____
_____

P: Personal Prayer:
_____
_____
_____
_____

E: Expression Through My Life (Action Step):
_____
_____
_____
_____

About the Author

J. K. Sanchez – Author, Graphic Designer and Publisher

J.K. grew up in Las Vegas, but fleeing the heat, she and her husband escaped to the Pacific Northwest almost four decades ago. Her savored moments are those spent with her husband – the love of her life, as well as her children, grandchildren and great-grandson. With two dachshunds at her feet, her days are active as she spends her retired time saturated in her passions of photography, gardening, growing flowers and of course writing.

As an author and photographer J.K.'s love for people and nature is portrayed both through visually descriptive prose (Devotional Studies in Nature vs. Spiritual, non-fiction short stories, Inspirational essays and teachings) as well as through the eye of the camera. Her spiritual passion for worship and the presence of the Lord draws her continually to see freedom proclaimed and released to others through the finished work on the cross of Jesus.

As an author, her works include:

A four book devotional series:
   Winters Rest (2014),
   Spring's Assurance (2015),
   Summer's Delight (2015),
   Fall's Yield (2015)

Inspirational collections:
   Reflection of His Glory (2015),
   Unearthing His Treasures (2019)

Multiple journals and a Prayer Journal (*Access to the Throne* (2017))

An inspirational collection of true stories written with 20 additional authors (Oh My God You Are Really Real (2018))

as well as contributor to (Keeper of the Faith (2016) and contributing author in Guideposts Angels on Earth Mar/April 2019)

As a photographer she has participated throughout Washington in gallery events and fairs, has photographed weddings, memorials, children, pets and personal portraits.

She currently has a published CD of her graphic landscape photographs (Names of God (2016)) as well as having contributed photographs for (Keeper of the Faith (2016) and (Unearthing His Treasures (2019)).

Titles available by J.K. Sanchez

Majestic Reflection Devotional Study Series:

Winters Rest

Spring's Assurance

Summer's Delight

Fall's Yield

Stand alone or companion journals:

Winters Rest Journal

Spring's Assurance Journal

Summer's Delight Journal

Fall's Yield Journal

Majestic Reflection Journal

Reflections of His Glory Journal

Oh My God You Are Really Real Journal

Additional Titles

Reflections of His Glory

Access To The Throne! – A Prayer Journal

Oh My God You Are Really Real

Unearthing His Treasures

Her books are available on amazon.com as well as J.K.Sanchez.com

She is also available at
facebook.com/authorJKSanchez
facebook.com/majesticreflections
facebook.com/JudyKSanchezPhotography
And don't miss her current blog at
unearthinghistreasures.wordpress.com
Email: jksanchez.author@gmail.com

Contact me at: JKSanchez.author@gmail.com

Jksanchez.com   Also find me on Amazon

www.ingramcontent.com/pod-product-compliance
Lightning Source LLC
Chambersburg PA
CBHW060515100426
42743CB00009B/1323